WASHINGTON'S HEADQUARTERS AT VALLEY FORGE

A Biography of a National Shrine

WASHINGTON'S HEADQUARTERS
AT VALLEY FORGE
A Biography of a National Shrine

James R. Bachman

Copyright © 2018 by James R. Bachman

All rights reserved.

ISBN 978-1-9757-8495-9

Printed by
CreateSpace Independent Publishing Platform

Cover photograph by Jeffrey Buehner

To Hulda

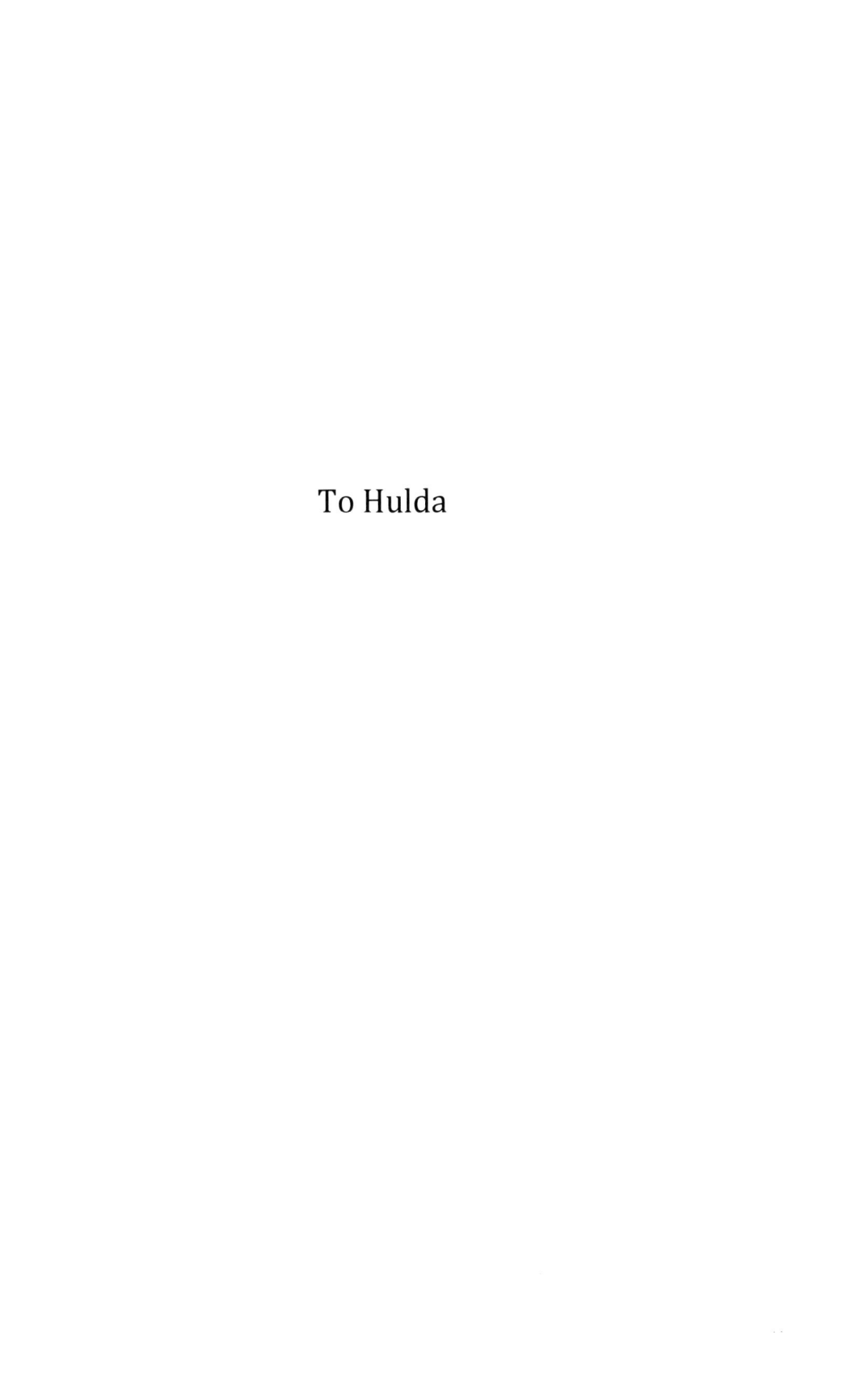

The Harder the Conflict, the Greater the Triumph

George Washington

About the Author

James R. Bachman, a professional historian, earned his doctorate at the University of Rochester. His personal interest in 18th century Georgian architecture and its adaptation to early American architecture led him to a study of Washington's Headquarters at Valley Forge, Pennsylvania.

He currently resides with his wife in Estes Park, Colorado.

Acknowledgments

My initial research on this work dates back some years, but other commitments deferred progress until recently. The early foundations were laid by the generous assistance of officers of Valley Forge National Historical Park. Especially noteworthy were the then Park historian, Joan Marshall Dutcher, historian Lee Boyle, and Phyllis Ewing of the curatorial staff. I should also give tribute to the tireless assistance of the archivists who brought to light indispensable documents and photographs.

In the recent phase of my work, members of the Valley Forge Park have been most generous with assistance through reviewing and offering directions on my emerging manuscript. The Chief of Interpretation, Jonathan Parker, kindly channeled the subject matter to Scott Houting, historian and Interpretive Park Ranger who is an authority on early Valley Forge and the Revolutionary period. Mr. Houting made indispensable suggestions and insights. Dona McDermott, a Park archivist, kindly proof read my book in draft and contributed needed commentaries and suggestions.

The recent full-scale resumption of the project owes much if not all to the inspiration of our friend Carol Kirkstadt, whose direction and technical expertise have been invaluable.

Two photographers, my nephew Jeffrey Buehner, and our friend Michael Cerwinka, provided artistic views of the inside and exterior of the headquarters house.

My earlier manuscripts had the benefit of scrutiny by my historian friend, Bruce F. Pauley, who provided many suggestions.

Two other friends, Nan Abbiatti and Susan Hackmeier, expended time and labor in proof reading the nearly completed manuscript.

Last but never least, every step of the process involved the faithful and tireless counsel and labor of my wife Hulda.

To all the foregoing benefactors, past and present, goes my boundless gratitude.

James R. Bachman
Estes Park, Colorado

Table of Contents

About the Author	
Acknowledgments	
Preface	1
Chapter One: 18th Century Matrix	5
Chapter Two: War Comes to the Valley	25
Valley Forge, Spring 1777 - December 1777	
Life during the Encampment	
(December 1777-June 1778)	
Chapter Three: The Potts House, a Study	60
Exterior Features	
Interior Features	
Joinery	
Paneling	
Structural Details	
Chapter Four: Ownership - First 100 Years	98
The Fate of the Wing	
Chapter Five: Public Ownership &	
Restoration Activity	125
Epilogue	173
Chronological Highlights of	
Headquarters Events	175
Notes	178
Selected Bibliography	185
Illustrations	189
Index	195

PREFACE

In a pristine river valley 20 miles west of Philadelphia stands a prim 18th century house which hosts hundreds of thousands of visitors each year. Its attraction is that it domiciled George Washington during some of the darkest days of the American Revolution. Washington slept in many structures during his career; some still stand, and a few were associated with other famous personages of that day or later. The Valley Forge house is far from the most famous, imposing, or elegant of these survivors, and its owners were not otherwise distinguished in national affairs. It is strictly the fortunes of war and the stature of a Commander in Chief that have bestowed renown and, very likely, preservation upon a tiny, two-storied stone dwelling on the right bank of the Schuylkill River.

So, an accident of history has bequeathed to our time an architectural jewel with an inherent interest and appeal. It is an aesthetic delight, emblematic of a long lost world of taste and patient craftsmanship. The foot-and-a-half thick walls and the classic wood paneling in the four main rooms witness to a time when skilled artisans routinely expended prodigious time and effort for patrons who expected it. The architectural details still please our eyes, and, as a representative building from any era, it can enlighten us on the life, ideals, and preferences of an age which, though once very real, now exists only in our imagination.

Washington's Headquarters in Valley Forge National Historical Park

In the more than two centuries since the army evacuated in 1778, George Washington's headquarters has survived vagaries which make its post-revolutionary history instructive in itself. It was in private hands for the first century, and while its association with the father of the country was always known, it received little special care. At that, it fared somewhat better than Mount Vernon, which had gone nearly to ruin before it was rescued in the mid 19th century. Yet, the Valley Forge milieu was not always sympathetic. One owner denatured the kitchen wing for his own family's convenience which, of course, he had every legal right to do. Nonetheless, the essential structure was never altered beyond recall.

The second century saw a succession of private and public efforts to preserve and to restore it to the exact conditions of Washington's visit. Attempts at restoration have not always been well-directed. A maddening dearth of early documentation has left much room for scholarly conjecture and some ill-considered action. This is especially striking in the treatment of the overwrought kitchen wing. Since the 1970s more sophisticated investigative and archeological methods have been applied to earlier mistakes. But it is never possible wholly to retrieve that which was lost. A copy is not an original. The task is not made easier when it cannot be fully known just what was lost.

But the basic fabric remains. The first century did not permit the Potts house to perish through neglect or abuse; the second did not manage to kill it through kindness. It is an old truism among historians that every generation to some extent recasts the past to suit its own preconceptions and desires. As this biography will show, the truism is no less applicable to the stewardship of an architectural relic. The quest for authenticity is bedeviled by illusions as well as ignorance. The quest must continue. One can hope that what greets the visitor to the Potts house today is reasonably faithful to 1778. The hope must bear the caveat that responsible scholars of the past were equally certain that their now rejected restorations had brought back the real thing.

However historically faithful the headquarters may now be, what stands is lovely. This short history honors the simple beauty of the house and sketches some features of the time which gave it form. Beyond that, it follows the vicissitudes of the building's post-revolutionary experience and, finally, celebrates the fact that it has survived.

CHAPTER ONE

THE 18TH CENTURY MATRIX

In spite of a large amount of historical information and imagination it would still be impossible for the modern visitor to Valley Forge to envision life in the Schuylkill River Valley as it was in the 1770s.

After a bewildering welter of roads, miles of commercialism and the complexes of corporate headquarters and motel chains, the Park will offer respite in a quiet enclave of the past. It is peaceful and spacious with its green hills and neatly pruned clumps of woodland. The clusters of rude, reconstructed huts sit just a bit incongruously upon the rural landscape. Westward from the visitors' center on the North Gulph Road, Mount Joy looms to the left. After the top of the ridge, the Great Valley and the Schuylkill River come into view, in all their splendor. The headquarters house once was visible from this point, but is today hidden by trees.[1] From here the descent is rapid. Near the headquarters house is a meadow plain in the foreground and dense stands of timber beyond. Overlooking this scene is the headquarters house itself, the impeccably restored little stone structure, standing dignified and aloof. In this gardenlike setting it seems that nature was sculpted just to provide a fitting museum for an architectural treasure.

Aerial view of Valley Forge - 2018

In fact, the Park is an idealization of the past, a necessary contrivance by its custodians to insulate it as far as possible from the alien hurly-burly of the modern world. The contrivance is a fiction. It tells little about the Valley Forge of the 1770s, which was by no means insulated from its world. It was then a vigorous commercial and manufacturing hamlet and was to become increasingly so in the early years of the next century.

The modern scene does not bring to mind the iron forge, grist mill and saw mills with their dams and waterwheels, the acrid odor of smoldering charcoal; the heaps of firewood in the muddy woodlots; the sweating draft animals with wagonloads of pig iron or wooden casks of grain; the roads which were no more than rutty paths that became quagmires from melting snow or summer rains; the men sweating in the forge or toiling on the surrounding farms with implements that would have been familiar in the time of Abraham; or the rafts laden with wood and foodstuffs floating down the river toward Philadelphia. The elemental, earthy nature of life in that time, on all levels and in all places, is perhaps hardest for the contemporary mind to conjure up.

Rude or not, Valley Forge's environs in revolutionary times had long since ceased to be a frontier. The region of Pennsylvania was well-settled by those of English ancestry, along with a sprinkling of Scots, Ulstermen ("Scotch-Irish"), and Germans. Immediate to Valley Forge were many families of Welsh background who still held to the patronymic, that is, the practice of taking a father's first name as the surname of his son (a practice which still survives in Iceland; quaint, but a genealogist's nightmare). Religiously, Quakers were still highly visible among the farming gentry, merchants, and middling sorts. Yet, sizable pockets of Anglicans, Presbyterians, Baptists, and German Lutherans lent a diversity which was already identifiably Pennsylvanian and previewed the eclectic denominational landscape of the later United States.

The economy of the countryside was also diversified. Original woodlands had retreated from the level, more fertile areas. Even on the hillsides the forests had been extensively cut over because of the insatiable demand for firewood. The revolutionary army denuded the neighborhood of timber. Farms in the locality averaged under 200 acres. Wheat and rye were the main cash crops. Fruit orchards were plentiful, their harvest being mostly for local consumption. Farms rarely had more than six to eight livestock. Pastures were of poor quality, consisting mostly of woodland or fallow fields, so animals were entirely for household use. But regions such as this having easy access to rivers developed commercial ties with Philadelphia, a little over 20 miles downriver. So, a happy confluence of water transport, water power, and plentiful firewood encouraged industrial hamlets like Valley Forge.

Neither was diversity lacking in the political sphere when the Revolution arrived. Philadelphia, the queen of colonial cities, a metropolis of perhaps 40,000, produced more than its fair share of loyalists, although many of them discovered the true depth of their devotion to crown and scepter just when the British General William Howe and his army occupied the city and appeared to be winning the war. Loyalism was not uncommon in the backcountry, even splitting families like the large and prominent one of Potts. But the British considered the rural regions north and west of Philadelphia as hostile territory, so they commonly committed raids against property in those outlands. Iron forges and mills were especially vulnerable, for they were associated with aid and comfort to rebels.

Most business enterprise in the 18th century was individual, family, or clan. Partnerships were commonplace means to amass sufficient capital to purchase land, to construct a small fleet of commercial boats, a metal forge, or a mill. Acquired capital was the motive force, the necessary foundation for a business venture; large-scale borrowing against future enterprise had to await a later day. The elaborate web of business collaborations was reflected in family connections. Intermarriage was routine. Among ironmasters of the Schuylkill River Valley, matrimonial liaisons between the Potts, Rutter, and Savage families effected a near monopoly of the industrial wealth of the area.[2]

The Potts family entered affairs of the Valley Forge only after the mid 1700s. The property adjacent to the Valley Creek and the Schuylkill River was part of the original Penn family tract, a landed reserve which had been retained for personal distribution by the proprietor. In 1742, a 175 acre tract was bought from the family by two business partners, Stephen Evans and Daniel Walker. The purchasers were soon joined by a third partner, and in 1743, an iron works, the Mount Joy Forge, named after the mountain just east of the Valley Creek, began manufacturing. It was a refining forge, designed to convert raw pig iron into bar iron from which straps, horse shoes, hinges, and nails could be made. Mount Joy Forge was not a success. By 1757, two of the partners had died, and Daniel Walker sold his third to Abraham Williams. The remaining two-thirds were then acquired by John Potts who, by various contrivances, soon possessed the remaining third. So during 1757 he became sole owner of the tract and its forge. John Potts (1710-1768) and his brother Thomas (1720-1762) were sons of Thomas Potts (1680-1752), who owned a pioneering iron works called Colebrookdale Furnace.

A descendant of John Potts and historian of the family, Mrs. Thomas Potts James, described John as the

> *largest and most successful iron-master in the American colonies, carrying on forges and furnaces, not only in Pennsylvania, but Virginia.*
>
> *He lived in great dignity at his stately house called Pottsgrove, surrounded by his large family of sons and daughters, and connected by birth and marriage with many of the oldest and most important families in Philadelphia.*[3]

The family, with its marital connections, was a prominent clan among the commercial gentry of the middle colonies.

Potts Family Crest

Thomas Potts Family

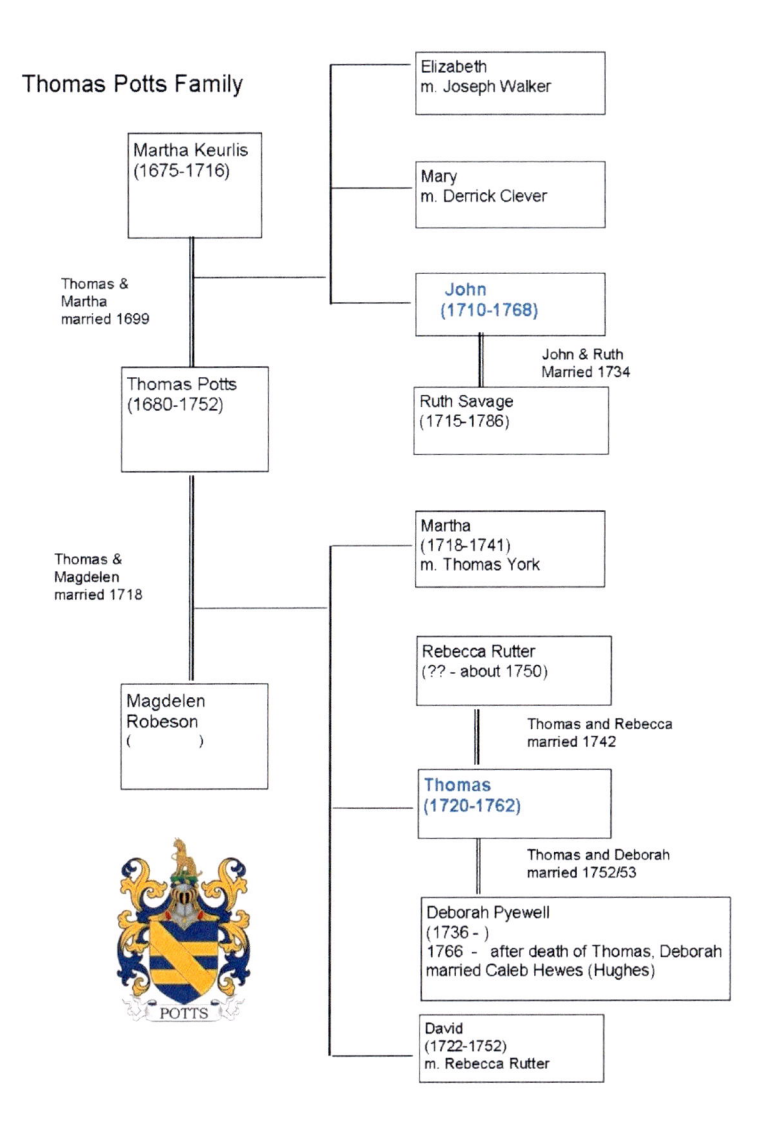

- **Martha Keurlis (1675-1716)** — *Thomas & Martha married 1699* — **Thomas Potts (1680-1752)**
  - Elizabeth — m. Joseph Walker
  - Mary — m. Derrick Clever
  - **John (1710-1768)** — *John & Ruth Married 1734* — Ruth Savage (1715-1786)

- **Thomas Potts (1680-1752)** — *Thomas & Magdelen married 1718* — **Magdelen Robeson ( )**
  - Martha (1718-1741) m. Thomas York
  - Rebecca Rutter (?? - about 1750) — *Thomas and Rebecca married 1742* — **Thomas (1720-1762)** — *Thomas and Deborah married 1752/53* — Deborah Pyewell (1736 -) 1766 - after death of Thomas, Deborah married Caleb Hewes (Hughes)
  - David (1722-1752) m. Rebecca Rutter

POTTS

Immediately after taking possession of Mount Joy Forge in 1757, John Potts sent a crew of supervisors, craftsmen, and laborers to begin repairs on the forge and construction or reconstruction of adjacent buildings and dependencies. The iron forge lay on the Valley Creek about 350 feet south of the point at which the Gulph Road to Philadelphia (now Highway 23) forded the Valley Creek. A dam some distance up the Valley Creek diverted water into an artificial channel (race) which led to the wheels providing power to the furnaces. After the water was dumped back into the Valley Creek, it soon confronted a second dam, this one just south of the road. It directed the water into a second race leading to a saw mill about 500 feet to the north, that is, downstream closer to the Schuylkill River.

Late in 1758, Potts' workmen began construction on a grist mill which straddled the saw mill's tailrace, so that the saw mill's tailrace became the mill race for the grist mill. The house owned by one of John Potts's younger sons, Isaac, which became Washington's headquarters, would nearly have faced the grist mill, although it is now thought that it was not built until some years later. The grist mill was a commercial fixture, raising revenue through custom grinding of wheat for neighborhood farmers as well as providing cheaper flour for the forge community.[4] The area north of the road and adjoining the Schuylkill River, containing the mills just described, would soon be legally distinguished from the remainder of the Potts holdings.

John Potts Family

John Potts (1710-1768) & **Ruth Savage (1715-1786)**

- Thomas Potts (1735-1785) Married Anna Nutt (1737-1796)
- Samuel Potts (1736-1793) Married Joannah Holland
- John Potts (1738-1810) Married Margaret Carmick
- Martha Potts (1740-?) Married Thomas Rutter
- David Potts (1741-1798) Married Mary Aris
- Joseph Potts (1742-1804) 4 wives
- Jonathan Potts (1745-1786) Married Grace Richardson
- Anna Potts (1747-?) Married David Potts
- Isaac Potts (1750-1803) Married Martha Bolton
- James Potts (1752-1803) Married Anna Stocker
- Rebecca Potts (1755-?) Married Dr. Benjamin Duffield
- Jesse Potts (1757-?) Married Sarah Lewis
- Ruth Potts (1759-?) Married Lehra

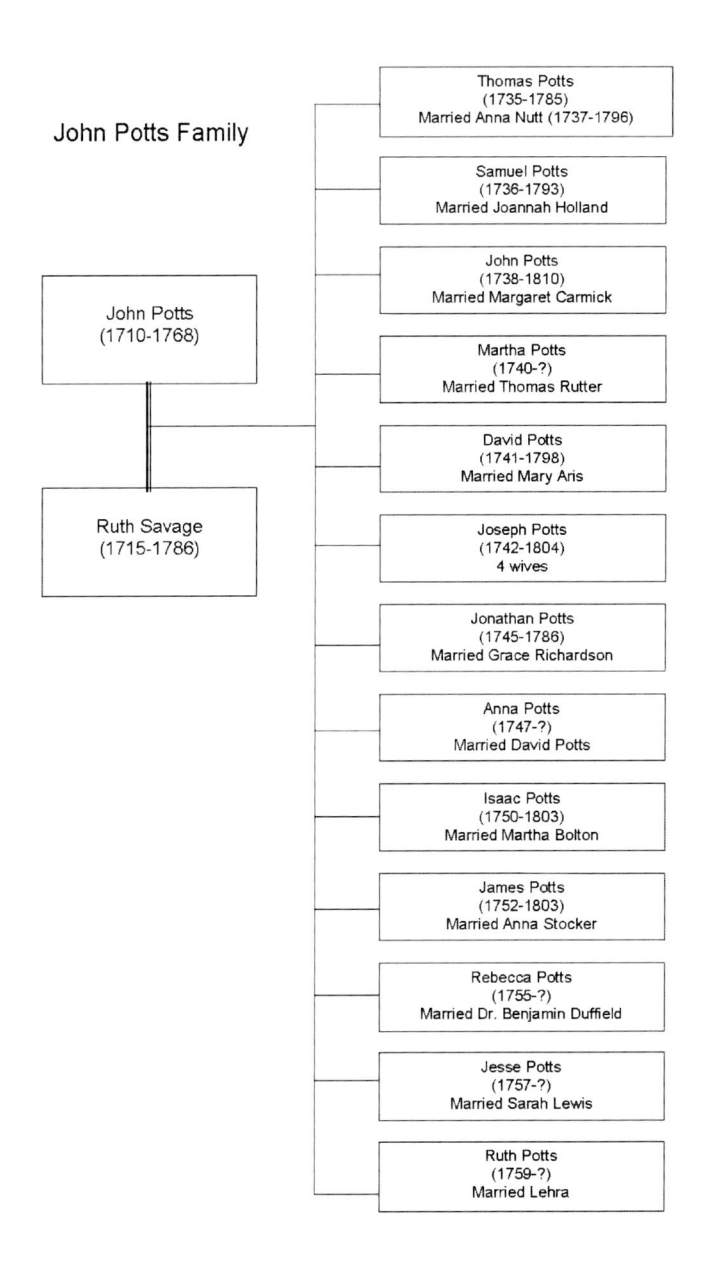

Through the ten years of his ownership, Potts left the running of the forge and mills to various partnerships of his sons, specifically Samuel, Thomas, John, David, and Joseph, as well as some relatives. After the mid '60s, he came to grips with the involved business of parceling out his estate to his extensive brood. In 1765, he bargained an agreement with his sons Samuel and John, by which they would purchase the Mount Joy Forge as well as their father's share in a furnace elsewhere. But by 1767, when John Potts executed his will, the arrangement had not been carried out. By this time it is probable that his son John was the most intimately involved in day-to-day operation of the forge, for Samuel was serving in the Pennsylvania assembly as representative from Philadelphia County.[5]

Some items of the will offer glimpses of social values and household concerns of that time. Potts was nothing if not direct:

> And the reasons why I have given my sons John and Jonathan less than my other sons is on account of the extraordinary expenses I have been put to for their education, & I have given my sons more than my daughters being of opinion that as sons they are justly entitled to more.

(The two sons mentioned were educated in Scotland, Jonathan becoming a physician. John remained a loyalist during the Revolution, for which he suffered confiscation of his property). Five other sons, including

Isaac, received a dispensation of £250 over and above their respective shares of the paternal estate. As for the family slaves:

> It is my will and I order that my negroes shall not be sold at public sale but appraised and divided among my children or to such of them as shall agree and choose them.[6]

The will described the section of the Mount Joy Forge property north of Gulph Road (containing the saw and grist mills) as a separate segment:

> Whereas I stand seized of a certain grist mill in the County of Philadelphia known by the name of the Valley Mill and of a small piece of ground thereunto belonging bounding and described as follows, Viz: beginning at the Valley Creek where the Great Road crosses it, thence along the same road towards Philadelphia by the gardens to the fence of the field on the north side of the said road thence along the said fence between the garden and said next Schuylkill and thence up the barnyard fence through the field to the middle of the old orchard in the hollow, thence by a straight line to Schuylkill thence up Schuylkill to the mouth of Valley Creek to the place beginning.[7]

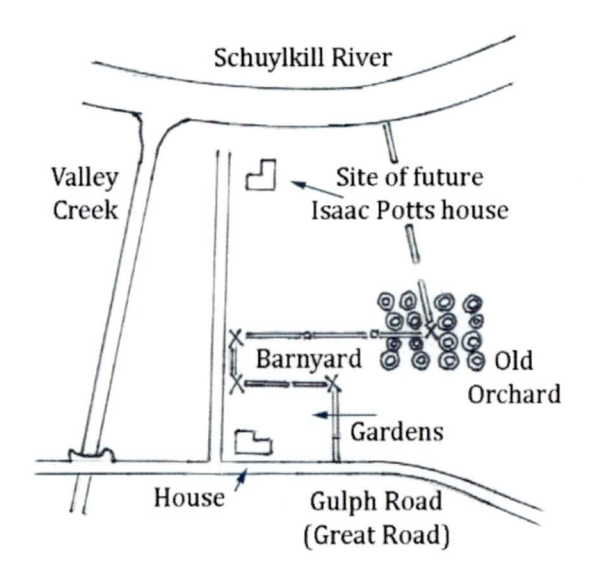

John Potts' Mill Tract property north of Gulph Road

In the spring of 1768, John Potts the elder granted to his son and namesake, John Potts, all of his Great Valley holdings. The next day, this son deeded back to his father the segment north of the Great Road, which included the 14 acre tract above described, i.e. the saw mill and grist mill tract. On the 10th of May, John deeded to his brother Joseph, a Philadelphia merchant, the ironworks and attendant tracts as well as the mill plot he had previously turned back to his father. Finally, the elder Potts made a gift to Joseph of his title to the mill property. Having completed the disposition of the Great Valley estate and his many other holdings in a timely manner, John Potts the elder made his worldly exit on the 6th of June, 1768. The motivations behind the elaborate transfers of title just described can only be guessed.

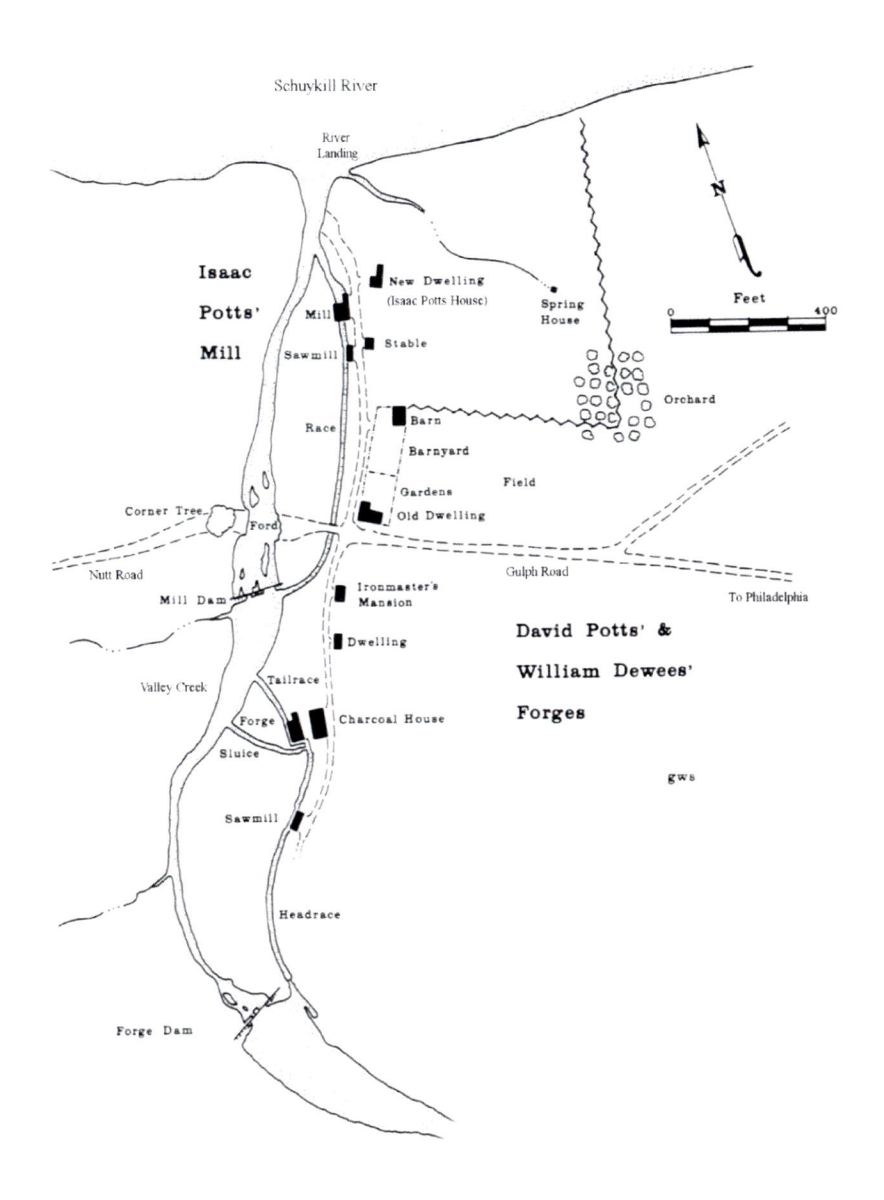

Valley Forge prior to the Revolution

But family claims on the Great Valley properties were to remain fluid yet awhile. Joseph continued to attend to his affairs in Philadelphia, while management of the valley iron works was carried on by another brother, Thomas, and a cousin. Isaac had charge of the grist mill operation after 1768, that is, from his 18th year.[8] To all appearances, Joseph was an ambitious enterprizer whose appetite for property soon outran his resources. By 1773, he found it expedient to reduce commitments and sold the 14 acre segment containing the mills to his brother Isaac, whose share of the inheritance from his father enabled him to buy the parcel outright, along with a tract near Pottsgrove.

The structures known to have been on the mill tract were the grist mill, saw mill, a barn, and a building just north of the Great Road and east of the Valley Creek which had been expanded and remodeled when John Potts acquired the property in 1757. The last seemed for a time to have been a boardinghouse for forge workmen.[9] It is mentioned as "old dwelling" on the map of Valley Forge prior to the Revolution. Sometime after the Revolution it became the property of David Potts who remodeled it into a dwelling for himself.

On the purchase agreement of the 27th of September, 1773, Isaac was granted the right to enter Joseph's tract south of the road to maintain the mill dam and race which provided water for his mills. The legal language defined Joseph as "gentleman," Isaac as "yeoman."

Below is an excerpt of the agreement:

> Whereas the said Isaac Potts is possessed of certain mills on the Valley Creek near Mountjoy Forge which for a considerable time after the forge stops working hath not a sufficient supply of water. Therefore the said Joseph Potts for diverse considerations doth hereby grant and covenant that the said Isaac Potts shall have the privilege of drawing the water out of the forge race after the forge stops working on the seventh day until 12 o'clock at night provided he shuts or causeth the gates to be shut at that time, which if he should omit or neglect to do that, this privilege is fully to cease or otherwise, if there is not water enough in the Valley Creek to fill the forge dam against 12 o'clock first day night, or if the owner or owners of said forge should build a dam at the head of the present forge dam in that case also, this privilege to cease....[10]

Almost simultaneously, Joseph Potts liquidated the rest of his Mount Joy holdings, selling the forge lands (everything south of the road as well as a sizable parcel north of the road and east of Isaac's mill tract) to his brother David and a partner, their cousin William Dewees (1739-1809). As Dewees had married Sarah Potts daughter of Thomas Potts and Rebecca Rutter in

1764, he had already been involved with the family for some years in iron manufacturing. He and David had operated the valley iron forges since at least 1771. They held equal shares in the forge property and the buildings upon it. From 1773 until the Revolution, they jointly set forth on vigorous development of the business, nearly doubling their landed property through acquisitions of additional woodland to feed the hungry furnaces. Dewees was apparently on the spot during this period and well into the Revolution. He personally managed the forge, while David was in Philadelphia marketing their wares.

Isaac was exclusively concerned with the mills during this period, but his specific activities are uncertain. A recent theory about his house, the future headquarters, is that it was built about the time he acquired the mill tract in 1773, furnishing him a domicile immediately adjacent to the mills. If so, he would probably not have actually occupied the house much before the Revolution. Devout Quakers, Isaac and Martha Potts had been members of the Radnor Quaker meeting in the vicinity of Valley Forge. Yet, in 1774 they transferred to the Exeter meeting, which indicates that they moved to the Pottsgrove area where Isaac indeed had also purchased some land. In 1773 he paid the taxes on his mill, but in 1774 they were paid by Dewees.[11]

Establishing a construction date for the Isaac Potts house is thus, by definition, speculative. It is unlikely that he would have had a substantial homeplace built just before departing the environs, unless the move was occasioned by unforeseen circumstances. In his absence he would most likely have left a foreman to run the mills or have leased them. But so finely detailed a house would hardly have been constructed simply to house a foreman or lessee. Could the dwelling have been built in earlier years, perhaps well before Isaac was even involved?

Until quite recently, earlier building dates had been assumed. Lorett Treese in her history of Valley Forge says "Washington's Headquarters was believed to have been built around 1760, but current thinking suggests it may have been built as late as 1773."[12] Mrs. Potts James was of the opinion that it was built in 1759.[13] But the description of the mill property in John Potts' will, noting other existing structures, makes no mention of the house. A more plausible period of possible construction would be 1768 to 1770, a few years before Isaac owned the ground. In this case, the house might have been intended for family use, perhaps on a periodic basis. Isaac's older brother, Samuel, had a house built near Pottsgrove in 1769, strikingly similar in form and detailing, suggesting that the same craftsman built both, perhaps sequentially.[14]

In the absence of documentation, architectural analysis has been recently applied to the building itself in order to fix its period. Such analysis is always complex, for nearly every structure exhibits features which were the "latest style," combined with others which were throwbacks. Such is the case of the Potts house. The closed string stairway is typical of the midcentury as is the fielded paneling of the fireplace walls. The unembellished doorways with headlights (transom) and the stark, cantilevered hood over the front door resemble those on other dwellings of the neighborhood erected in the 1750s and 1760s. These details could easily corroborate 1757-'59 as construction dates and certainly the pre-1768 period.

Southeast view showing chimney caps

But other features suggest a post-1770 date. The twin chimney arrangement did not appear before the

1770s. Prior to 1770, dual end chimneys were merged before reaching the roof peak. The circular window, or oculus, in the south gable would only have been found in a far more palatial house before 1770. Similarly, the vertical alignment of the oculus, upstairs window, and first floor doorway was peculiar to the 1770s and after. Chapter Three, The House, will analyze the architecture in more detail. But the substantive information conveyed by the house itself suggests that it was built after 1770, making the acquisition date of the mill property by Isaac Potts a most plausible time.[15]

What appears to be firm documentary evidence recently came to light, proving that the house existed by 1776 and that Isaac was living in Pottstown. On February 7, 1776, this advertisement appeared in "The Pennsylvania Gazette":

> To be lett for one year, and may be entered the 1st day of the fourth month next. A convenient two story stone house, with a kitchen adjoining, also a good garden, stables, & etc. Situated in Upper Merion Township, Philadelphia County. For terms apply to Isaac Potts, Potts-town or David Potts, Philadelphia.[16]

As the house was not immediately available, it was probably occupied at the time of the advertisement, but not by Isaac.

It is conceivable that a Mrs. Deborah Hewes rented the house at this time or shortly thereafter. The advertisement does not appear again. She was the occupant at the time Washington appropriated the house as his headquarters and who signed the receipt for the 100 English pounds compensation. In 1776, she was living in Philadelphia with her second husband, a hatter named Caleb Hewes. An earlier assumption that she was again a widow in 1777 was erroneous, but the whereabouts of Caleb at the time is unknown. If he had been present during the summer of 1778, he, rather than his wife, would likely have signed the receipt. In 1782, Caleb was living at Pottsgrove with Deborah, pursuing his trade as a hatter.[17]

    Deborah's first husband had been Thomas Potts, brother to John Potts the elder, so she was an aunt by marriage to Isaac. However, she had a number of other familial connections to the Potts family. Although he was living at Pottstown during these years, it is possible that Isaac made frequent visits to Valley Forge to look after his mills, but this is purely speculative. It is almost inconceivable, given the crowded conditions of the headquarters, that Deborah and at least two young children by her two marriages would have remained at the house during the encampment. With numerous relatives in the immediate vicinity, she would have had no difficulty finding refuge.

CHAPTER TWO

WAR COMES TO THE VALLEY

VALLEY FORGE, Spring 1777 through December 1777

In the spring of 1777, Commander William Howe and the British army were in New Jersey near present-day Perth Amboy. Washington and his ragged Continental army were encamped at Morristown, in watchful waiting. General Washington assumed that Philadelphia was the logical objective of Howe's spring campaign. It was the nerve-center of the revolution, the meeting place for the Second Continental Congress. Indeed, Howe, having failed to obliterate Washington's Army and thereby crush the rebellion during the previous fall, could think of nothing better than to add Philadelphia to the list of outposts now liberated from treason, a list which included New York City. Loyalists were reputed to be a dominant element in Philadelphia, despite the presence of the Congress and an obstreperous party of rebels. Some British agents assured Howe that he would be welcomed with open arms.

Washington anticipated that the assault on Philadelphia would be from New Jersey across the Delaware River. He was disturbed at the number of

American military stores stowed in Philadelphia and its environs, which could easily be seized by invading redcoats. For some months he urged Congress to move them to more remote backcountry locations.

In early March one ostensibly remote spot was visited by the Continental Army's Quartermaster General, Thomas Mifflin. The spot was 20 miles "back" of Philadelphia, an iron forge and cluster of buildings in the Great Valley of the Schuylkill River, a place already referred to as the Valley Forge. At this time the forge was operated by its half-owner, William Dewees, who had become a colonel in the Pennsylvania militia. His partner and cousin, David Potts, was marketing the wares produced at the forge from his residence in Philadelphia. Mifflin informed Dewees that he had decided to establish a supply station at the forge because of its secure location and the available structures.

Dewees was not pleased, complaining that the cache might make the forge community a target of British wrath. Mifflin assured him that the distance from the Delaware River was too great for the British to be a real threat, and, in the off-chance that they should come, the valley could be easily defended or the supplies be moved out before the enemy's arrival. Dewees was far from satisfied, but found himself shouting into the wind. Not only did Mount Joy Forge (Valley Forge) become the unwilling repository of the quartermaster stores, but of the commissary supplies as well. Dewees yielded most reluctantly, and in only a few months his apprehensions were to prove well founded.

By August of 1777, Dewees noticed that some of the flour in the commissary store was going bad. When he notified the Board of War, he was given the honor of selecting six bakers from his militia who, upon being granted furloughs, were assigned to baking the flour into bread. It was long thought that Dewees had ovens built in the basement of the former rooming house for forge workers, but research has shown that to be untrue. Wherever the ovens were located, Dewees' bakers converted unstable flour into very stable "hard biscuit" to feed hungry solders.

The course of the war demonstrated that Valley Forge was not the secure, backcountry refuge it was earlier thought. The British Commander Howe's grand strategy to capture "the rebel capital" Philadelphia had been worked out by the spring of 1777, after his thrusts into New Jersey had failed to bait Washington into open combat. Howe was a cautions man. A march overland across New Jersey risked overextended communication lines and rebel ambushes. He decided instead on an elaborate seaborne expedition designed to deceive. In the summer, the Commander pulled his troops back to New York and loaded over 15,000 men on a fleet of 260 ships and set sail. A fraudulent secret dispatch indicating that the armada was heading for Boston was "allowed" to fall into rebel hands hoping that Washington would rush his army back to New England. Washington was not deceived.

Military logic would at this time have ruled that Howe move his forces rapidly up the Hudson River in order to meet General Burgoyne's expedition coming south from Canada toward Albany, a strategy earlier agreed upon to separate New England from the rest of the rebellious colonies. But General Howe was no slave to logic. When he heard of the capture of Fort Ticonderoga, he concluded that Burgoyne could get along without him. In July, Howe appeared in Delaware Bay, so it was clear that Philadelphia was his goal. He could now sail up the Delaware River to Philadelphia, or land his ship-weary troops at any point for an easy march on the capital city from the south. But so obvious a move would have risked encountering Washington, who, Howe learned, had not traveled north with his army to counteract Burgoyne. Moreover, reports indicated that strong rebel forts lined the Delaware River between the British force and Philadelphia.

     Thus, another clever deception was in order, a surprise attack on Philadelphia from a different angle, through the "back door." The fleet put out to sea again. Howe hoped that this would trick Washington into thinking that Philadelphia was no longer threatened and that a southern campaign or a rush northward to join Burgoyne was the real British plan, the appearance at the Delaware River being merely an elaborate ruse. Howe's scheme nearly worked. Washington had decided that the enemy was indeed headed for the Hudson River and made preparations to march his own troops northward when he got word that the British had landed at the head of Chesapeake Bay. While this demonstrated that Philadelphia was the target, it also gave some hope to the Americans. It showed that Howe and Burgoyne were not about to coalesce into one grand army of conquest.

Howe's maritime strategy had once seemed so rational to him. To ship his army by sea would prevent the debilitation of a land march during the hottest season. But the six week confinement to shipboard in withering heat exhausted the patience and health of the soldiers. Most of the horses died from heat, thirst, or hunger. When the landing did take place, Howe was only a few miles from where he had been, in Delaware Bay, three weeks earlier. Philadelphia was a bit farther away now and there was still Washington to confront. Ironically, if Howe had landed only a few days later, Washington might already have marched north, leaving Philadelphia undefended.

What had been gained? Nothing at all, but much had been lost. In mid June, Howe was 20 miles from Princeton, about 60 miles from Philadelphia. On the 24th of August, he was still 60 miles from Philadelphia and much farther from his base of operations in New York. Moreover, His Majesty's great victory campaign of 1777 had been set behind more than two critical months. This would not have mattered much if Howe could now confront Washington and obliterate his army in one decisive engagement. Such a consummation was devoutly wished by Howe, for it would totally redeem his badly tarnished reputation. Washington, who also desperately needed a dramatic victory, rushed south from Philadelphia to meet him.

In reality, the stage was set for another prolonged interval of frustration for both sides of hardship, near-disaster, and political rancor. On the 11th of September, Washington confronted the British at Brandywine Creek but was driven back, badly outgeneraled by Howe and his able subordinate, Charles Cornwallis. After losing several hundred men, Washington escaped to Chester on the Delaware River, and then retreated northward toward Philadelphia, crossing the Schuylkill River and resting only a day at Germantown, a few miles northwest of Philadelphia. This left the British nursing their wounded and consolidating their position in the region south and west of the Schuylkill River.

On the 14th of September, Washington re-crossed the Schuylkill River, eager for another confrontation with Howe, and moved west along the Lancaster Road (now Highway 30). He ordered the fortification of several fords on the Schuylkill River to plug up as many potential British crossing spots as possible. On the 15th of September, when he heard that Washington had re-crossed the Schuylkill River and was apparently positioning himself to block a British move over the river against Philadelphia, Howe got his army marching northward toward nearby West Chester to prepare for battle.

Location of military operations, fall 1777

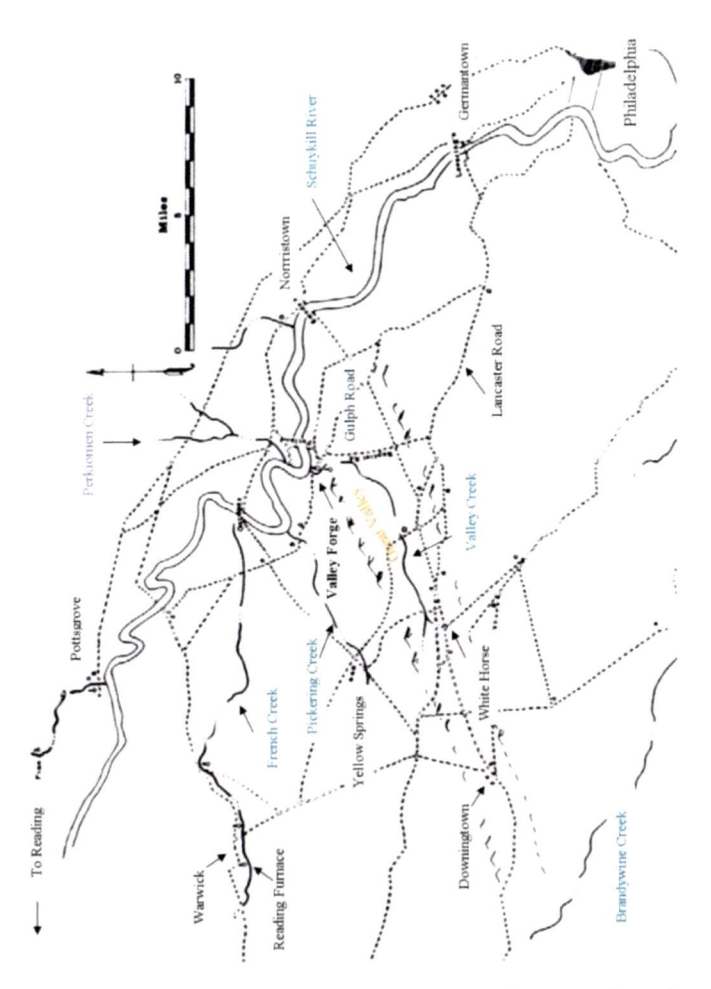

Seeking as usual to avoid a head-on confrontation, Howe struck toward Washington's right in hopes of pinning the rebels against the Schuylkill

River. By the 16th of September, Washington had arrayed his soldiers on the crest of the hills forming the southern boundary of the Great Valley. On the verge of what could have been a decisive battle, a deluge drenched the combatants and rendered Washington's forces helpless. Because of cartridge boxes which were not waterproof, the American powder was ruined. Washington retreated westward to Yellow Springs as a refuge to get his army and ammunition dried out. By the next day it was obvious that resupply was imperative, so he continued the retreat to Warwick and Reading Furnace. At this location, new supplies could be had from Reading, north across the Schuylkill River, the depository of stores which had lately been hastily evacuated from Philadelphia. Washington's challenge was now to anticipate Howe's next move: west against Reading and Washington or east against unguarded Philadelphia.

It should be noted that all of this activity was in the immediate neighborhood of Valley Forge, so the forge and its rebel supply depot could hardly have remained immune from the tumult. On the day of the aborted battle, Washington directed his chief of the army's baggage, Clement Biddle, to move the baggage on to Yellow Springs. Finding the direct routes clogged, Biddle had to detour north to the Great Road (or Gulph Road) through Valley Forge. As he had probably been authorized to do, Biddle called on Dewees to get an inventory of the supplies. On the evening of September 16th, Biddle wrote the Commander in Chief:

I have stopped at this place ... to examine the state of the stores at this place and I enclose to your Excellency an estimate hastily taken from the Gentleman in charge of them which he says may be incorrect – I have desired him to procure boats and teams to haul them to the landing (not 400 yards from the Stores) and as he complains that his hands have all been taken from him who did this business, I have taken the liberty to assure him that any persons employed in the Service should be exempted from militia duty while engaged therein.

Estimate of Store at Valley Creek forge
Tuesday Evening, ¼ after 8 o'clock 16 Sept: 1777

> Qu: M: Gen: Stores and Forage
> 3000 bushels wheat part ground
> 20,000 tomahawks or rather more
> 5,000 sets horse shoes
> 3 or 400 axes helved and ground
> A great quantity of spades, shovels and pick axes
> 4 or 3 tons Barr iron
> 20 or 30 Cask Nails
> 6 or 700 camp kettles
> A number of other articles of less value not included in the above

Commissary Stores
2,000 barrels flour
1,000 w bread which with some of the flour is to go off

> to the Army at the Yellow Springs in the morning with five wagons - - boats are ordered and wagons to haul them to the landing as early as possible and col. Biddle has directed them to the east side of the Schuylkill.
>
> Wm Dewees, Jr.[1]

Biddle departed that evening and, once again, poor Dewees was to have an onerous responsibility dumped upon him without adequate help to carry it out. Washington ordered the baggage under Biddle's authority be sent immediately westward to Warwick; the baggage and ammunition at Perkiomen Valley Creek (across the Schuylkill River and a short distance upriver) should be forwarded to Pottsgrove. Washington also ordered his generals, Maxwell and Potter, to see that the supplies at Valley Forge were moved out as expeditiously as possible. For some reason, the generals did not get the orders or misinterpreted them, for Dewees and a small band of assistants were left alone, unaided and unprotected, to move the supplies out. This they were doing by loading the stores on rafts constructed for the purpose and ferrying it bit by bit across the river. Meanwhile, on the 18th of September, British forces under Wilhelm von Knyphausen and Cornwallis, which had begun an eastward march toward Philadelphia, camped only three miles due south of the forge. The setting was right for another American disaster, and it soon came.

A British scout came across the frantic activity at Valley Forge. With a cooperative local resident as guide, three companies of light infantry rode north on Baptist Road. The most direct route from the British encampment to the forge would have been through the hills on each side of Valley Creek, but there was then no road paralleling the Creek. Upon reaching the Gulph Road, the British moved left over the rise on the flank of Mount Joy and descended swiftly upon the industrious rebels in the valley below.

This brought the desperate effort to save the supplies to an abrupt end. Colonel Alexander Hamilton, fresh from Philadelphia where he had warned the inhabitants – especially the Continental Congress – that the British were coming, had shortly before arrived to assist in the evacuation. Colonel Henry "Light-Horse Harry" Lee was approaching from the west on Nutt Road (which connected with the Gulph Road at the Valley Creek) with a troop of Light Dragoons when the British fell upon the scene. Hamilton and Lee concluded that they were outnumbered and that discretion was the better part of valor. Under a hail of shots, Lee and his men retreated in the direction whence they came. Hamilton, Dewees, and helpers escaped across the river by barge, also under fire. Colonel Dewees' horse was shot, but there were evidently no human casualties. Valley Forge was at the mercy of the British. A Captain John Montresor noted in his journal that they took possession of a rebel depot of

3800 Barrels of Flour, Soap and Candles, 24 Barrels of Horse Shoes, several thousand tomahawks and Kettles and Intrenching Tools and 20 Hogshead of Resin.[2]

On the 19th of September, the premises were flooded with British troops and officers. Cornwallis and his column marched past the forges and camped just to the west and across the river from Perkiomen Valley Creek where the Americans were now situated. Washington had crossed that very day at Parker's Ford about eight miles upriver. The British Light Infantry began removing the stores at the Valley Forge. The main British army was now ready also to move to Valley Forge, but first a threat to its rear must be dealt with. An American detachment under Anthony Wayne had secreted itself at Paoli to harass the British from behind. On the night of the 20th of the same month, the British assaulted Wayne's camp, eliminating many Americans by the bayonet alone in the infamous "Paoli massacre." Howe was now ready to make his crossing of the Schuylkill.

On the 21st, the British Army moved to the Schuylkill River, encamping itself from French Creek to Fatland Ford. Washington feared that Howe was preparing to move westward against Reading, a vital American depot. Howe wanted Washington to think this very thing and made preparations for another elaborate deception. Upriver from the forge, conspicuous work on a bridge was begun near the mouth of Pickering Creek, convincing Washington that Howe was looking west.

Washington fell back to avoid attack on his right flank. On the 22nd, Howe made two feints, at Gordon's Ford and Fatland. But early on the 23rd, Howe reversed, marched his army back through Valley Forge, crossed at Fatland Ford and marched eastward toward Philadelphia. Washington was far to the west and in no position to intercept him. Howe's ruse had worked and Philadelphia was defenseless. The British made their triumphal entry on the 26th of September, with fifes and drums sounding, flags flying, and crowds of Tories cheering their arrival. One week earlier, the Continental Congress had made its hasty departure for the west country, establishing headquarters-in-exile in Lancaster and then York. By the 26th, Washington and the army had settled into encampment up the Perkiomen Creek at Pennypacker's Mill, today Schwenksville.

But before leaving Valley Forge, the British did not fail to leave their calling card. They no doubt thought it important both to punish Dewees for his support of the rebellion, which included harboring enemy supplies, and to make certain that the forges and mills not be used again in behalf of the Continental Army. Casks of gunpowder were stacked against the dam and ignited. The dam was destroyed, releasing a cascade of water. The forge and dependencies were put to the torch. When Washington and the army arrived in barely three months, these structures were charred ruins. Fortunately, residences were apparently spared, including a relatively new stone house overlooking the mouth of the stream and the Schuylkill River.

These were bitter days for Washington and the revolutionary cause. The series of defeats in the field; the Paoli massacre; desertion and discontent in the ranks; the constantly nagging supply problem – in no way mollified by the Valley Forge fiasco; growing dissatisfaction with and criticism of Washington's generalship; and now, the loss of Philadelphia. Washington no doubt swayed between discouragement and despair, for he was subjected to an upswell of attacks on his military competence and even his character. The pressure made it imperative that he produce a spectacular battlefield victory, never mind that just since the battle at Brandywine Creek his army had dwindled to barely over 13,000 men. Germantown came so frustratingly near to satisfying this demand.

Howe divided his forces between Philadelphia and Germantown, a village a few miles northwest of the city. This unwise arrangement invited attack and inspired Washington to make a lightning assault which commenced in the early hours of the 4th of October. In the initial phases, the ferocity and effectiveness of the rebel attack were so great that the British were forced to retreat nearly in a rout, suffering heavy casualties. Howe scolded his scurrying troops for flinching before what he believed was only a "scouting party," but the Commander himself beat a precipitate retreat after nearly receiving a load of grapeshot.

The Americans were exultant in their early successes, sating their appetite for revenge of the "Paoli massacre." Washington's minions could have chased the disarrayed British right into Philadelphia, but some tactical errors soon aborted the emerging triumph. There was no help from a tenacious fog which hampered communication and even caused the Americans to fire upon each other.

The major tactical error was storming the Chew house. Beside the thoroughfare of the American advance stood the stately stone mansion of Justice Benjamin Chew. It was occupied by a company of British who used it as a fort from which to fire upon the passing Americans. The choice for the American command was either to neutralize the fort or detour around it and press on in pursuit of the main British force. Henry Knox, Washington's able subordinate, had read too many European military manuals which warned against leaving a castle in enemy hands at one's rear. He convinced Washington to capture the Chew house, an effort which proved bloody, time-consuming, and futile. Artillery was brought up, but six pound cannon balls bounced off the thick walls.

The hours' delay for what was probably a needless exercise proved fatal. Washington's forces lost their momentum, giving the British a chance to re-form and launch a counterattack. As order was breaking down among his ranks, Washington saw no alternative to ordering withdrawal. His exhausted army marched in good order to Whitemarsh and from there back to the starting point at Pennypacker's Mill.

The battle of Germantown was less important for its actual outcome than for what it almost was: a smashing American victory. Some tactical deficiencies were all that prevented this, but far more significant was the demonstration of what spirited and determined soldiers, however raw and ill-trained, could do against disciplined British and mercenary professionals. Washington's troops, in their zeal and idealism, nearly carried the day, and the fact was not lost on them or the enemy. The Americans saw Germantown as a disappointment but not a defeat. The British bewailed the heavy losses and were embarrassed that the Americans, whom they enjoyed viewing with such contempt, had given such a good account of themselves.

Nor was the event lost on an important foreign observer, the French foreign minister, the Count de Vergennes. He had urged his king, Louis XVI, not to ally with the Americans, for they could surely not hold out against British might. His conviction was shaken, not only by the clear victory of Horatio Gates, officer of the Continental Army, at Saratoga, almost simultaneous with the Germantown engagement, but by the rebel performance at Germantown. Both episodes persuaded Vergennes that the American cause might not be hopeless. The road was being paved for the French alliance a few months later.

With the deterioration of his army, Washington could see no chance of driving Howe's forces physically out of Philadelphia, even though some members of Congress believed that he should try to do just that. The best course was to use the rebel control over the hinterland to starve the British out. Critical to this were the two American forts just south of Philadelphia which blocked seaborne supplies coming up the Delaware River. But despite gallant defenses, both forts were in British hands by early November. Howe and his army were secure in Philadelphia for as long as they pleased to stay; warm, comfortable, and well-supplied. Washington's miserable and shrinking forces were dug in at Whitemarsh, only 18 miles away.

But Howe's obligation was to destroy the rebels once and for all; the pressure became relentless to do something climactic. On the 4th of December he marched out with 14,000 well-fed and well-equipped troops to confront Washington who could count no more than 7,000 men actually fit for duty. Yet the Americans were well-situated at Whitemarsh and virtually dared Howe to attack. As in previous instances, Howe overestimated the number of the enemy, so he stopped short of Whitemarsh at Chestnut Hill, hoping to lure Washington into the open field. Had he succeeded, he might well have wreaked devastation on the Americans. Washington wisely avoided the trap. After some skirmishes but no major engagement, Howe marched back to Philadelphia on the 8th of December and settled in for the winter.

With weather growing intermittently nasty, Washington now had to choose between listening to armchair patriots who urged him to liberate Philadelphia, or making a realistic appraisal of his army.

He followed the latter course, moving his exhausted, hungry, poorly-clothed, and somewhat dispirited men to winter quarters at Valley Forge. Thus began a six-month interlude in many respects more anxious for commanders, more psychologically wearing for the soldiers, and more trying for everyone's soul than the terrors of bloody battlefields.

The six month encampment was not in any sense a military confrontation, but it was a fateful struggle of epic proportions. The ability of the revolutionary army to prevail up to December, 1777, could so easily have been rendered meaningless during the subsequent half year. Morale was at a nadir. The shrinking of the pathetic army through illness, deprivation, and desertion seemed nearly inexorable. While contrary to romantic depictions, the winter was comparatively mild. That was little solace to soldiers ravaged by malnutrition, disintegrating clothing, and the torment of body lice. Washington's exasperation drove him nearly to resignation in the face of Congress' mismanagement and unresponsiveness, not to speak of a torrent of personal criticism and Washington's belief that a clique conspired against him.

By February and during intervals thereafter, almost any observer would have had to conclude that the game was over.

It might very well have been but for some fortuitous counterattacks against the gloom. The arrival of Baron von Steuben who drilled Washington's rabble into something like real soldiers (and raised morale in the bargain) set the stage for a resurgence of recruitments as spring came on. The talented work of Nathanael Greene as Quartermaster General meant that by early spring adequate clothing and food was available to the long-suffering troops. Admiration and respect for Washington had by late winter overwhelmed the detractors. Tom Paine had directed his deathless prose to gilding the Commander's image. By spring the friction between the latter and Congress had subsided. Lord Howe was relieved of his command in Philadelphia and replaced by Sir Henry Clinton. From London came renewed proposals for a cessation of hostilities and reconciliation. Immediately after this came the news of the French alliance with material promises of military support to the Americans. Even Washington's legendary composure was shaken by the joy that this report brought him. On the 6th of May, a service of thanksgiving, a military exercise and feast marked the

Baron Friedrich Wilhelm von Steuben, 1730-1794

celebration at Valley Forge. The impressive precision of the soldiery in their drill bore heartening witness to the achievement of von Steuben.

In the spring of 1778, the British high command recognized that the French warships bound for Delaware Bay would make British retention of Philadelphia impractical. Sir Henry Clinton was ordered to evacuate the city and convey the army back to New York by sea. He saw reasons to disobey orders: many loyalists, fearing rebel vengeance, wanted to accompany the British, and available ships were inadequate for both troops and refugees. Also, a sea voyage would be so slow that Washington might, by a land crossing, capture New York before Clinton's fleet arrived. On the 18th of June, at three in the morning, Clinton's army of nearly 20,000 and whatever loyalists had not already been dispatched by ship, crossed the Delaware River and set forth across New Jersey toward New York.

On that same day, Captain Gibbs, an aide to General Washington, paid Deborah Hewes 100 pounds, Pennsylvania currency, for use of her house and furniture. The army evacuated Valley Forge in hot pursuit of Commander Henry Clinton. It attacked the British in wilting heat at Monmouth, but it was an ineffective venture because of the bungling of General Charles Lee, whom Washington had reluctantly given command. The resultant disgrace, court-martial, and suspension ended the career of this vain and unsavory man. Clinton continued on to New York while Washington marched to northern New Jersey and the

Hudson River. The disposition of both armies was almost identical to what it had been two years earlier.

Over two years of struggle and disappointment were yet to elapse before the American cause would be victorious.

Peace lay over Valley Forge, strewn with an army's residue and nearly denuded of vegetation. To the residents of the spot, effacing the evidence of their visitors must have been a sole concern. Life had to go on, and it would be several generations before cherishing the immortality of their place would bear more weight with the dwellers than the impulse to forget, or to ignore.

LIFE DURING THE ENCAMPMENT

December 1777 to June 1778

Going into winter encampment was common practice in the 18th century. Moving armies about, even well-trained and well-supplied armies, was many times more difficult in rain, snow, slush, and mud. Bivouacking became a nearly insuperable problem when firewood was wet or nonexistent and supply trains were hard put to keep up with a mobile army slogging over rutty trails and fording swollen streams. The hardships broke spirits, illness and desertions increased. As the lethargic Lord Howe appeared content to avoid the trials of a winter campaign to enjoy Philadelphia hospitality and the arms of a Mrs. Loring, Washington saw many advantages in a respite for his bedraggled force. Perhaps the ill could be nursed back to health. Perhaps the crisis of supply could eventually be rectified. And perhaps his still ill-disciplined soldiers could get some much-needed training in the martial arts.

General George Washington and Marquis de Lafayette at Valley Forge

  A number of factors conditioned the selection of Valley Forge for the encampment. It lay on the Schuylkill River, a strategic route to the interior, and so any thrusts by the enemy could be quickly countered.

The river itself, to the north and east, was a natural protection. The ground on which the army camped is not a valley at all but a plateau paralleling the right bank of the river for about two miles. From the Valley Creek at the west end of the plateau, the elevation rises precipitately a couple of hundred feet to a ridge, which is a shoulder of Mount Misery and also abounds the Valley Creek. East of the ridge is the plateau which, with its heavily wooded slopes on all sides, was reasonably secure from surprise attack. Howe's intelligence informed him that as the rebels were dug in, a major assault against them would be extremely costly. The British remained in Philadelphia.

On the 12th of December, 1777, Washington set forth from Whitemarsh and crossed the river, marching a short distance to Gulph Mills. There the decision to occupy Valley Forge was made. During this period the weather turned quite nasty, with frost, snow flurries, thaw, rain, and more frost. With clothing and shoes literally disintegrating, marching became a torment for many soldiers. Washington made the observation that the army's route to Valley Forge could be easily traced by the bloody footprints. This sounds dramatic, but there may have been some truth to it. On the 19th of the month Washington and his troops moved into winter camp. In three weeks, Washington noted, 2,000 men had abandoned the army because of hardship and exposure, desertion and expiring enlistments.

With about 11,000 to 12,000 men remaining, "two thousand eight hundred and ninety-eight of whom were unfit for duty," as Washington stated, rapid housing was imperative. Washington ordered that the soldiers be divided into households of twelve each to cut trees and construct their own huts which were to be 14 by 16 feet, with walls 6 ½ feet high. A monetary reward would go to the first household to complete its shelter.

Huts at Valley Forge

Hundreds of windowless log huts, the estimate is approximately 1300 to 1600, soon arose on the bleak hills, their cracks chinked with clay. Fireplaces were also built of wood and plastered with clay on the interior. With seasoned firewood nonexistent, fires in the huts produced far more acrid, choking smoke than heat.

Washington remained in a large canvas tent for the first five days while his soldiers erected their hovels. Even in his drafty marquee, the Commander was confronted by a mass of paperwork and correspondence. The loyalist John Potts, Jr. requested that his wife and children be given safe passage (presumably from Pottsgrove) to join him in Philadelphia and that he might also be permitted to move his household effects into Philadelphia. Washington responded:

Headquarters, Dec. 20, 1777

Sir:

In answer to your Letter delivered me by Major Jamieson. When Mrs. Potts applies she will have my permission for herself and Children to go into Philadelphia. As to your Household furniture, I cannot consent to their removal, they being under the cognizance and direction of the Legislature of the State. The bearer will escort you tomorrow morning as far as our Pickets.

I am etc.[3]

On Christmas Eve, with troops quickly providing shelter for themselves, Washington moved with his staff into the house owned by Isaac Potts, the small, two-story stone dwelling by the confluence of the Valley Creek with the Schuylkill River. The house was then being rented by Mrs. Hewes with perhaps two of her children. It is possible that her husband was there at this time as well, but he was apparently not present six months later when the army departed. The family presumably found refuge elsewhere. On Christmas Day, Washington dined with his officers at headquarters.

The military household was crammed into the four-and-a-half room house with kitchen wing attached. There was a basement and attic, but only the unheated attic would have been used as quarters for a servant or two, along with the luggage which may have been stowed there. The attic or garret was no more than five feet high. The "effective" indoor space would have totaled barely over 1,100 square feet, including hallways. Washington's major officers eventually found lodging at other houses in the vicinity.

The actual number occupying the little house can only be guessed, but there is no question that conditions were crowded. In addition to General Washington were the members of his military family, which lodged in the house at the constant beck and call of the Commander. The usual complement was a staff of eight, six regular and two special aides. It was generally a young group, ambitious and zealously committed to the revolutionary cause. Among the regulars were Alexander Hamilton, aged twenty, later prominent in the Constitution controversy and as President Washington's first Secretary of the Treasury; John Laurens, twenty-three, a volunteer aide and South Carolinian whose father was president of the Continental Congress; and another volunteer aide, Tench Tilghman from Maryland. The two special aides were Caleb Gibbs, a Rhode Islander, and George Lewis, Washington's nephew from Virginia.

This group had responsibilities comparable to any general staff; keeping records of financial accounts; transmission of dispatches to and from their chief; making arrangements for accommodations; handling matters of military discipline; and - nearly incomprehensible to a later age of abundant mechanical aids – the massive correspondence and copying of orders and other official papers, entirely in longhand.

In 1778, the "military family" was only the beginning. On the 5th of February, Martha Washington joined her husband and remained until the 9th of June. Her presence brought a feminine touch to the congested, barracks-like headquarters. She oversaw social amenities for which her husband had little or no time, receiving and entertaining a remarkable stream of visitors as well as the wives of other officers. She could also oversee the servants, a task for which long experience in managing the Mount Vernon household had prepared her.

There were at least eight and possibly as many as ten servants. The General was attended by his body servant, William "Billy" Lee; a steward supervised household supply and the remaining servants which included the cook, Black Isaac, a housekeeper, Elizabeth Thompson, and a washerwoman, Peggy Lee. Sundry other retainers took care of the horses and equipment. A steward during the early part of the encampment, Patrick McGuire, proved to be unacceptable, as explained in Washington's letter to his aide, Thomas Warton, Jr.:

He was hired about twelve months ago, to act as Steward in my family which station he continued until a few weeks past, when I was obligated to dismiss him, and I have the greatest reason to believe, that during the whole time of his employ, he took every opportunity of defrauding me. He is given to liquor, and where he dare take the liberty very insolent.[4]

The fact that he was not replaced after his dismissal in March suggests that Lady Washington may have taken over the steward's responsibilities for the time being.

Map of Encampment at Valley Forge by Louis Duportail

For all of the correspondence and other written records produced during the encampment, frustratingly little is revealed about the headquarters house. In fact, there is not much beyond legend to prove that the Isaac Potts house was the headquarters. The most concrete evidence are the several maps drawn at the time of the encampment, all of which indicate headquarters on the traditional site. A map drawn by the French engineer, Louis Duportail, even outlines a house with wing as headquarters, a shape similar to the Potts house.

One other bit of evidence appeared in a letter from a later owner of the headquarters to Mrs. Potts James:

> ... an old Jonathan James, a Revolutionary pensioner, died in Valley Forge about 1830 or 1831, near ninety years of age, who told me he had seen the General and wife at this house, and turned wooden bowls for her which she took to Mount Vernon.[5]

In support of this meager documentation is the fact that nothing in popular lore even remotely challenges the authenticity of the headquarters.

Recorded comments during the encampment offer enticing hints about the house, but little more. In staff correspondence were several complaints about cramped quarters, crowded, noisy rooms, and other irritations. The most famous reference was in a letter from Martha Washington to a friend, Mercy Warren:

> ... The General's apartment is very small; he has had a log cabben built to dine in, which

has made our quarters much more tolerable than they were at first.[6]

This casual bit of information spawned the log cabin mystery which, as later chapters will show, hovered over the house for generations.

But in which room(s) did General Washington sleep, or have his office? His staff meetings? Where did Lady Washington sit while darning socks in company with other officers' wives, if indeed she did? Researchers have seized on clues, however subtle, for enlightenment. In April of 1778, four Quaker women visited the headquarters, seeking a conference with Washington. One of the women, Elizabeth Drinker, gave an account of the event in her journal:

> *Arrived at headquarters about half-past one o'clock; requested an audience with the general; sat with his wife (a sociable, pretty kind of woman) until he came in. A number of officers there, who were very complaisant - - Tench Tilghman among the number. It was not long before G.W. came and discoursed with us freely, but not so long as we could have wished, as dinner was served, to which he had invited us. There were fifteen of the officers besides the General and his wife, Gen. Greene and Gen. Lee. We had an elegant dinner which was soon over, when we went out with ye*

> *Gen.l wife up to her Chamber, and saw no more of him.*[7]

Lady Washington's chamber was obviously upstairs and a visitors' room for officers' wives after dinner.

One other reference to Martha's quarters and a shadowy hint of the house's anatomy is contained in a description by Elias Boudinot. Boudinot was an officer on Washington's staff, who described General Charles Lee's liberation from British captivity. On the 6th of April, Lee was received with great warmth by Washington and his retinue amidst military pomp.

> *. . . He passed thro' the lines of Officers and the Army, who all paid him the highest military Honors to Head Quarters where Mrs. Washington was and there he was entertained with an Elegant Dinner, and the Music Playing the whole time . . . A room was assigned him, Back of Mrs. Washington's Sitting Room, and all his Baggage was stowed in it. The next morning he lay very late, and Breakfast was detained for him. When he came out, he looked as dirty as if he had been in the Street all night, soon after I discovered he had brought a miserable dirty hussy with him from Philadelphia (a British sergeants Wife) and had actually taken her into his room by a Back Door and she had slept with him that night.*[8]

Vignettes of the house such as these have served to confuse speculators more than satisfy them, as further discussion of the headquarters floor plan will reveal.

A recently approved internal publication of the National Park Service, "The Furnishings Report" has proposed a probable use of rooms during the encampment.[9] The front room in the first floor may have been a combination aides' work room and, at least before the log cabin was built, a dining room. It could also have been a reception and/or waiting room for visitors. Such multi-purpose rooms put a premium on compact, portable, collapsible camp furniture. The back room is assumed to have been the General's office and staff conference room (a removable stool on one window seat has fueled generations of speculation about Washington's using the hidden cavity to stow secret papers).

On the second floor, the small hallway room was perhaps used for guests. The Park's "Furnishings Report" concluded that the main front bedroom was an aides' room, probably jammed with camp beds during the night. The largest bedroom, to the rear, would have been for General and Lady Washington; now, which would have been Martha's sitting room? This is nearly pure speculation. Elizabeth Drinker, the Quaker lady, indicated that it was upstairs. It could have been Martha's bedroom, but the Washington's bedstead would have dominated the space. Unless the beds were collapsible and removable, which is unlikely, the room would hardly have served as a place for the Lady to receive visitors. Moreover, as the Marquis de Chastellux noted a few years later: ". . . American manners do not admit of a bed in the room in which company is received, especially when there are women."[10]

So, the old idea that the front room was Mrs. Washington's sitting room may have been correct. The aides' camp beds were "struck" each morning, leaving the room free for Martha during the day.

If this is true, how does the arrangement correspond with Elias Boudinot's report on General Lee's shabby conduct? He mentioned that Lee was quartered in the room "back of" Mrs. Washington's sitting room. If the room to the rear of the house was the General's, the reference could only have been to the small hallway room. This is believable, but what "back door" did Lee use to spirit his live baggage in? The room has no back door, only one opening conspicuously into the hall. The house has at least two doors which could be called back doors, but neither of these would serve as secret passages for hussies, or anything else.

One can only conclude that (a) Boudinot's description was carelessly framed, or his information, if second-hand, was faulty; (b) the use of the rooms was different from that earlier described; or (c) some other house was being described. The first possibility (a) seems to be most plausible.

The episode of General Lee is hard to credit, given its remoteness in time and place, not to speak of

Boudinot's possible personal bias. In short, the historian earnestly seeking information about the headquarters as a domicile during the encampment must grasp at straws, and these straws are few and meager.

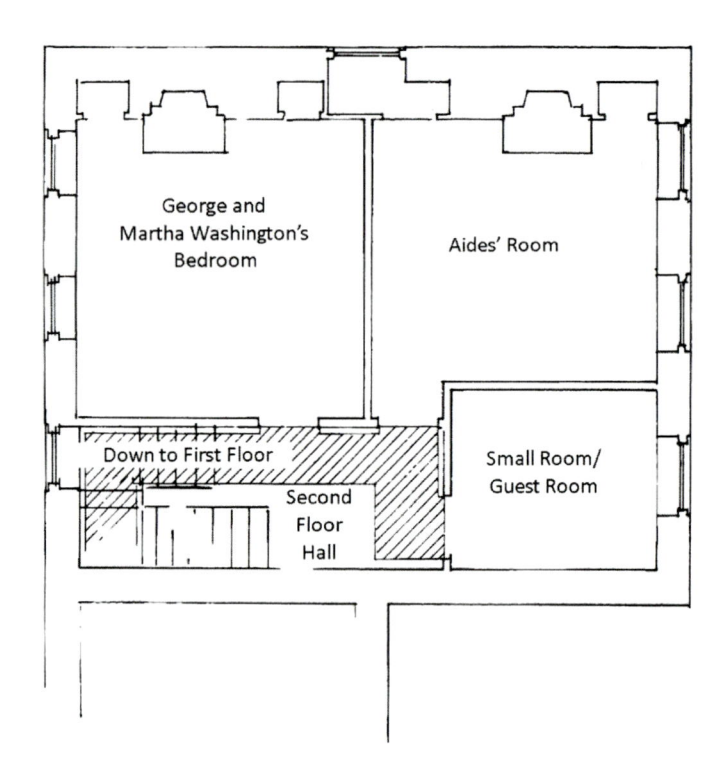

Washington's Headquarters - second floor plan

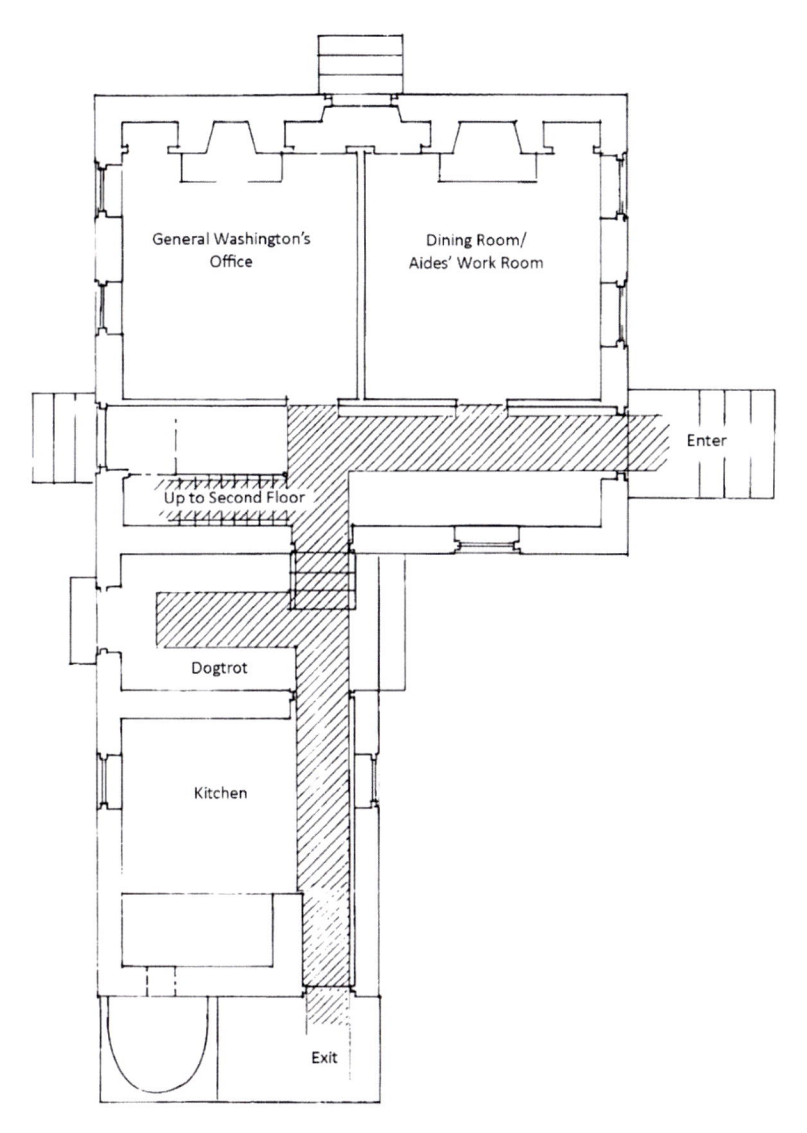

Washington's Headquarters - first floor plan

CHAPTER THREE

THE POTTS HOUSE, A STUDY

Nothing is known about who designed or constructed the Potts house. It was not likely conceived by an architect in a modern sense of the word but by a master builder familiar with a variety of basic designs which he could combine or synthesize for specific clients. The houses then built would be larger or smaller, more or less elaborate, but they nearly always followed "modern" style. That is, their layouts and details embodied the fashions of the 1760s, '70s, and '80s which the builders and their assistants were expected to have mastered. Since the master craftsmen learned the conventions from the same sources, other master craftsmen and English style books, the houses built for prosperous merchants in Massachusetts and Pennsylvania or landed gentry in the Chesapeake area and Carolinas all looked "late Georgian." Of course, there were regional variations in building materials as there were in taste. The unsupported hood over the entrance door of the Potts house is identifiably Dutch or Pennsylvania German.

Once builders had mastered the formalized layouts, canons of embellishment, and practical requirements, house design in that age was comparatively simple from our modern point of view. Fenestration (window placement), partitions, doorways, chimney location, and roof pitches were the sole concerns, matters strictly aesthetic and structural. No technical complications like heating ducts, wiring, plumbing, and bathrooms presented themselves. While it is known that some slipshod construction took place in the 18th century, most building of the time was substantial by virtue of what would today be called over-engineering. Houses were built to last simply because that was the way things were done.

The speculative use of the headquarters house during the military occupation evokes the congestion of a small domicile. But the owner and probably the builder envisioned the structure as a comfortable and proper dwelling for a highly respectable midsized entrepreneurial family. The parlor and dining room on the main floor served the formal functions of the family, and two full-sized bedrooms on the second floor, augmented by a small room, probably bedded down a substantial family, with some imagination.

The main body of the Potts house is a rectangle with exterior measurements of 25 feet, 4 inches by 30 feet, 4 inches.[1] The narrower dimension constitutes the west front (façade) and the east rear. The broader walls are the ends, surmounted by gables, meaning the axis of the roof ridge is parallel with the smaller dimension. This has not always conformed to formal canons of proper design, but the colonial and early federal periods abounded with examples of it. The plan, with its pinched façade, suggests a townhouse on a narrow lot, not a country house with abundant space. However, this too, was not an unusual arrangement in rural houses of the time.

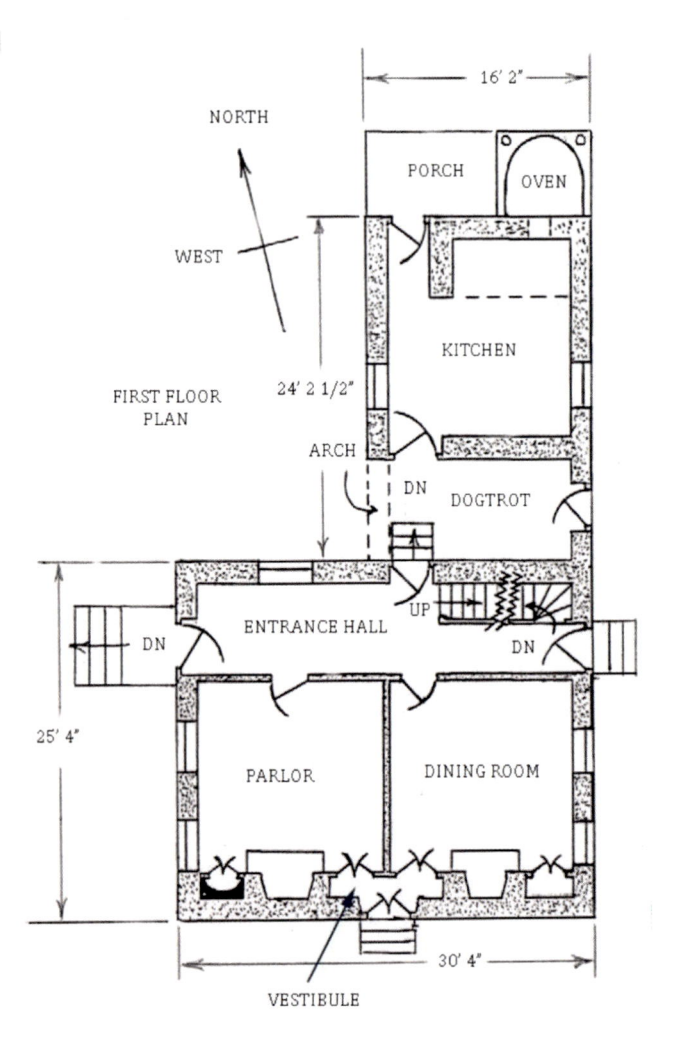

Drawing of Potts house – first floor plan

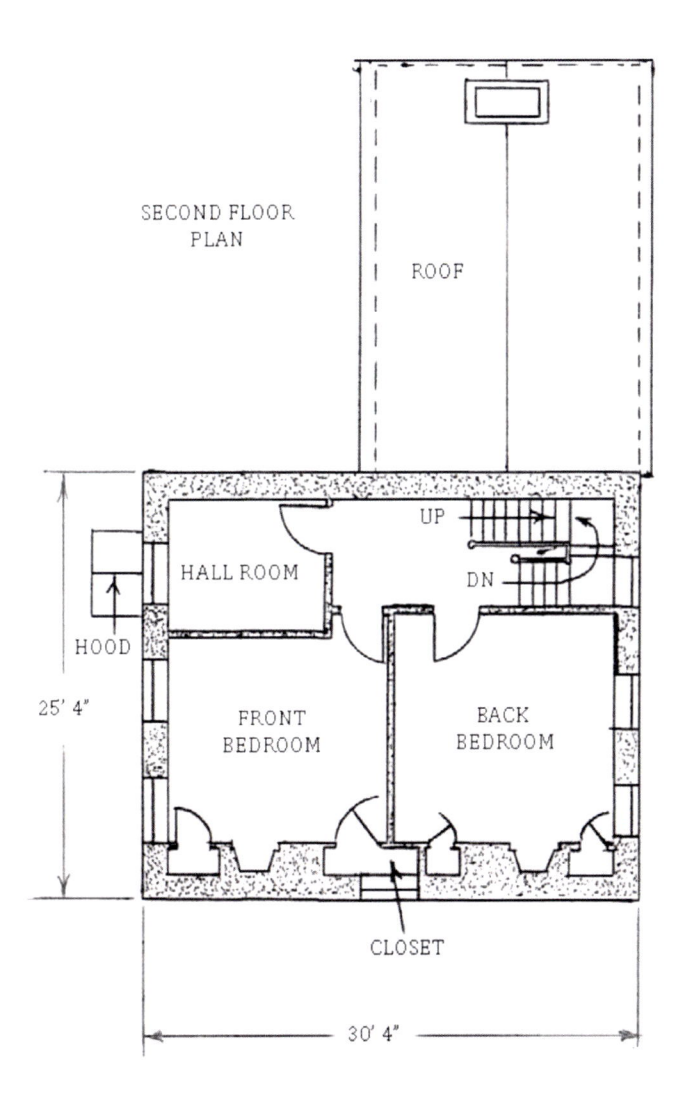

Drawing of Potts house - second floor plan

EXTERIOR FEATURES

The façade of the three-bay house with the large windows and hooded entrance door has a miniature elegance in no way suggestive of a humble country house.

Drawing of west elevation (façade)

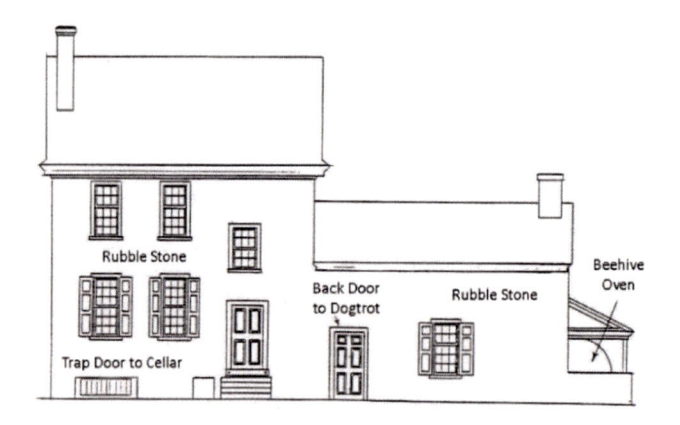

Drawing of east elevation (rear)

In the north end, after a set-back from the façade of 14 feet, a one-and-a-half story kitchen wing takes off. Its exterior dimensions are 16 feet, 4 inches by 24 feet, 4 inches. However, the kitchen's north-south exterior length is only 17 feet, 1 inch, for it is separated from the main house by a semi-enclosed breezeway, or "dogtrot." This area is open on the front, topped by a segmental arch which spans the entire 7 foot, 3 inch width of the dogtrot. On the rear, however, the dogtrot is enclosed by a solid wall, flush with the walls of the house and wing, broken only by a door.

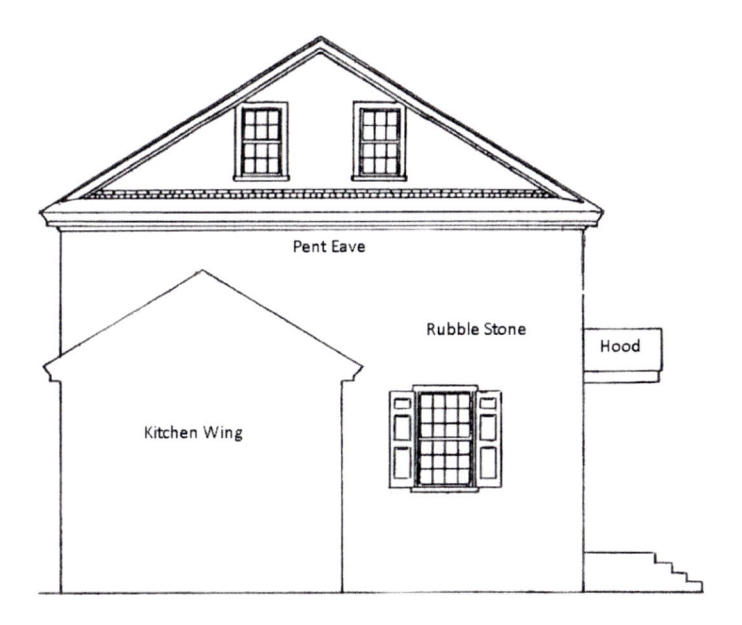

Drawing of north elevation

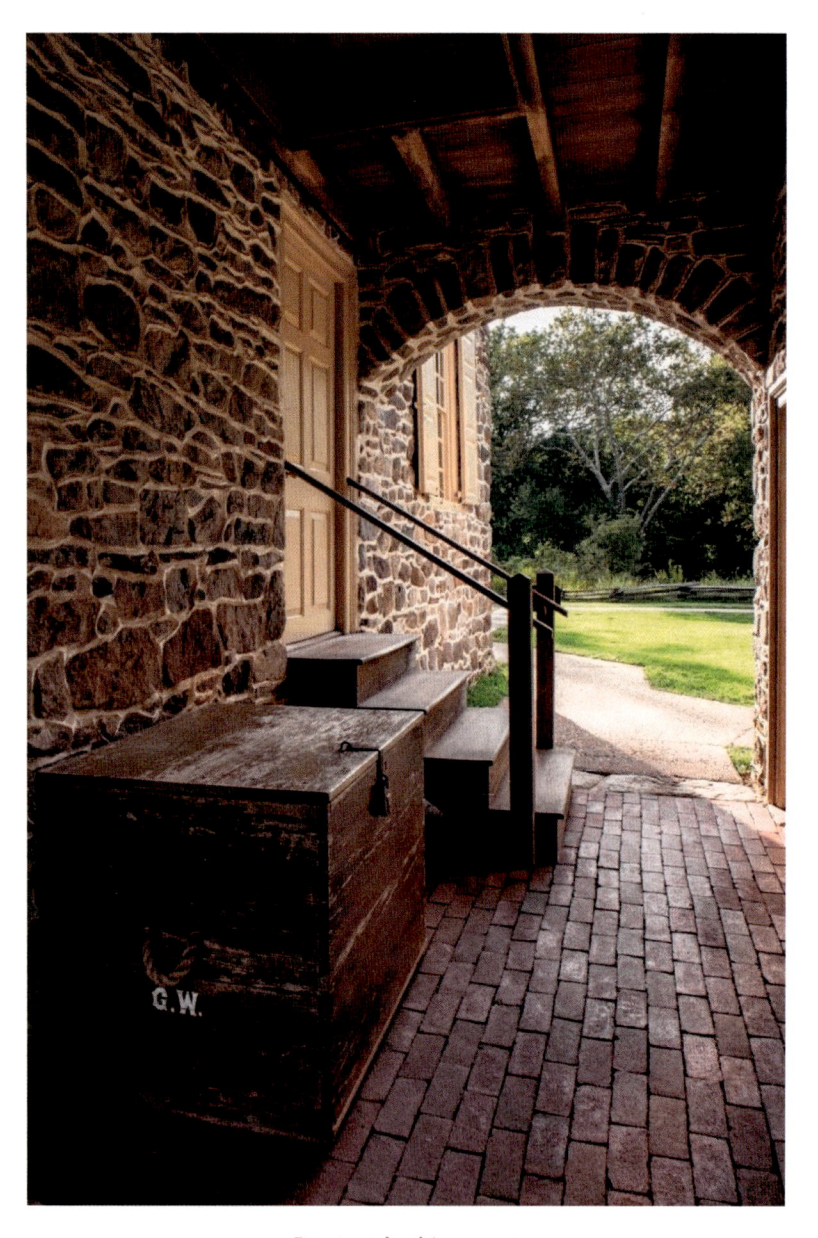

Dogtrot looking west

Separate or semi-detached kitchens were commonplace in the Chesapeake area and southern colonies where the heat of cooking, odors, and insects related to food preparation would be intrusive through many months of the year. In the colder climate of the middle and northern colonies, dogtrots were comparatively rare, although other examples exist such as the summer kitchen on the Peter Wentz house at nearby Worcester, Pennsylvania. The unusualness of this feature in a Pennsylvania dwelling has contributed to an ongoing controversy among restorers of the Potts house over more than a century. Unlike the main section of the house, the wing has been altered so often that little remains of the original workmanship and material.

Dogtrot at Wentz House

The south end is wholly symmetrical with the oculus, window and door flanked by matching twin chimneys. The gable and pent eave form something approximating a closed Palladian pediment. This is an ornamental triangular to a wall or portal based on the work of Andrea Palladio. Palladio was a 16th century Italian architect who adapted architecture from the ancient world. His work was much incorporated in architecture from the Renaissance to the 18th century.

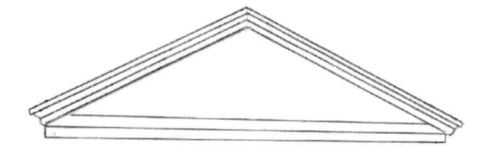

Drawing of Palladian Pediment

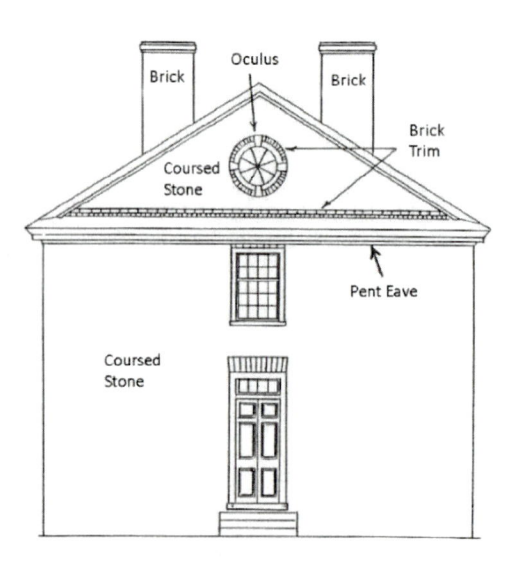

Drawing of south elevation

The pent eave, frequently but not consistently found on gables of the time, lends a formal, classical finish. It was also practical, diverting rainwater away from the porous stone or brick walls below.

Much of the beauty and character of the Potts house lies in the exterior walls, created from stone typical of its area. Eastern Pennsylvania, parts of New Jersey and the Hudson River region are blessed with rich strata of sedimentary rock which, when quarried, is ideal for building. The 18th century produced a bounty of skilled stone masons who fashioned thousands of mansions, simple farm houses, spring houses and barns, many of which still gladden the eye. Since weight and primitive means of transportation necessitated use of the material as close to its origin as possible, and since texture and color of the stone varied region to region, a trained eye can tell from a sample in what locality a wall was erected.

Although the walls of the Potts house look like granite, they are actually micaceous sandstone, lighter and easier to work than granite. It is multi-hued, ranging from salmon to dark purple. On the façade and south wall, the formal faces, the stone is coursed; i.e., the blocks were dressed roughly rectangular and equal in size, then laid in courses much like brickwork. On the back, north wall, and kitchen wing the stonework is called rubble. The original rubble still shows signs of coursing, but in the later, restored stonework the rubble becomes almost totally random. The walls average 18 inches in thickness, thicker near the base, thinner near the roof.

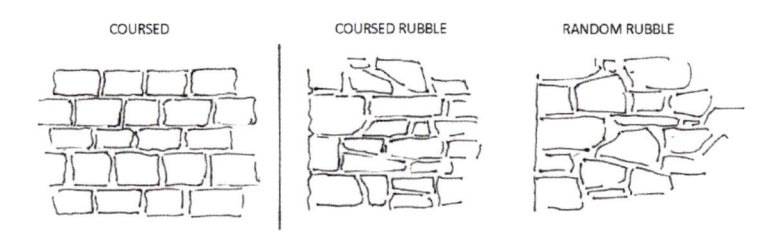

Drawing of stonework patterns

In a few spots the stonework is relieved by brick accents. The twin chimneys are brick, as are two courses immediately over the pent eaves and a course surrounding the circular window in the south gable. It is most likely that the soffit of the segmental arch over the dogtrot entrance was also originally brick. Brick was often used for boundaries around doors and windows in stone walls. It was not only a pleasing embellishment but made refined delineations easier for the mason. Stone is a coarser, more difficult medium to shape. On the other hand, on the lintels above the two front windows on the first floor, the south door and the window above, thin slabs of stone were set vertically to form flat arches.

A further word should be said of façades and architectural customs of that time. In a town house, the façade made sense; the best face was toward the street, its handsomeness impressing the passerby. Less care was spent on the sides and rear, leading to what has long been called a house with "a Queen Anne front and a Mary Anne behind."

While not a town house, the Potts home had a narrow façade that was nevertheless still a façade. The west front, with coursed stone and formal fenestration, was clearly its best face. It did not confront a major thoroughfare but a river access road to the Valley Creek and Isaac Potts' grist mill. How much traffic the road then bore is unknown, but it is hardly important. Contemporary canons dictate that a house have an identifiable façade, however situated. It could plausibly have been oriented toward the river as is the porticoed side of Mount Vernon, but in the Potts' case the river end (north) was the utility end. The land view was clearly considered more important.

This presumption is further suggested by the treatment of the south end. With its high visibility, it would have commanded attention second only to the west front, conceivably even more than the façade. So it was treated by the builder as a secondary façade with its regularly coursed stone, matched chimneys, formal pediment with oculus, and the flat arches above the door and window.

All physical evidence confirms that the main body of the house has never been significantly altered. The west entrance, beneath the hood, opens onto a hall which runs the full depth of the structure. The stairway takes off next to the north wall, its upper landing being immediately above the rear door. Just before the stairway on the north wall is yet another exterior door, this one leading to the dogtrot and thence the kitchen.

INTERIOR FEATURES

The two rooms on the first floor open to the right of the hall, a parlor or front room and a dining room to the back. Both rooms are about 13 ½ feet square with ceiling heights averaging just over nine feet.

Parlor showing door to vestibule

The south fireplace walls are fully paneled. Each room has a door in its paneling which opens onto a small vestibule leading to the outside through the south double door, frequently called a "carriage door."

It is possible that the carriage door would have been an alternative entry, perhaps even receiving guests alighting from carriages. But the inelegance of the vestibule and its opening directly into the rooms makes this unlikely. It is more likely that it was a service arrangement for such functions as stoking the fireplaces. The doors would also have provided ventilation in warm weather.

Dining room showing door to vestibule

The main bedrooms of the second floor closely duplicate the first floor layout. Their fireplace walls are also fully paneled.

The front bedroom is impinged upon by a small hallway room without a fireplace.

However, the front bedroom enjoys sole access to the second floor counterpart of the first floor vestibule, a small closet or secluded space flooded by light from the window on the south wall.

Closet is used here in its English sense, not to be confused with the modern Americanization of the word to mean a place to store clothing and other things. The English still refer to the latter as a "cupboard." The closet had a venerable heritage in the mother country, a solitary retreat from households in which children and servants made privacy scarce.

The recesses beside the fireplaces also provided cupboards. The cupboards behind the paneling in both rooms are small, and the shelving which fills the cupboards in the rear room suggest that clothing was as often folded as hung in that day. As earlier mentioned, the aides' room may have been the one used by Martha Washington as a sitting room. Lady Washington's services with visitors and supervising housekeepers probably rendered the effort of daily converting her room trouble well expended.

Second floor – front bedroom - (Martha's sitting room?)

Another view of second floor – front bedroom

Second floor -back bedroom

  Completing the main section is an attic and basement. The low-ceilinged attic, or garret, is partitioned into a north and south section, the south illuminated by the oculus and the north by two six-over-six windows. It is totally plastered, suggesting that it might have been used as a servant's quarters. Plastering of garrets was commonplace, for it provided some insulation and protected against fire hazards from open candles. There is no hearth. Meager warmth might have come from the two chimneys which project into the south chamber, but hardly enough for real comfort during winter weather. On the other hand, fires were infrequently lit even in bedchambers with hearths, except when they were used as sitting rooms or as sickrooms. What use was made of the basement is uncertain, but it was most likely for storage, especially of commodities that needed some protection from summer heat. The floor was earthen until 1976, when it was covered with concrete.

The first floor vestibule and second floor closet suggest recourses required by erstwhile design conventions. It is axiomatic that the architecture of formal buildings of the period put exterior balance and proportion foremost, molding interior arrangements to suit portals and fenestration. It is common to find elegant mansions with perfect symmetry in which inside stairways cross over windows. The tiny town house plan of the Potts house could show respect for the formal proprieties, especially on the large-windowed façade, with no internal disruption. The first and second floor room locations were congenial to the front and back window and door locations.

This was not the case with the south end. There was a logic in the twin chimney masses serving the four main rooms. Because of the smallness of the structure, it was necessary that these primary rooms be about equal in size. Yet, since the only place for windows or doors in the south wall was the center, partitions dividing the rooms from each other would necessarily split those apertures. As the shallow recesses beside the chimneys left only 20 inches between the paneling and the inside face of the outer wall, a purist of the time might well have adopted the tidy solution of totally omitting openings on the south, leaving a solid wall of stone. Such things were not at all unthinkable, even in country houses. Indeed, Mount Pleasant in Fairmont Park, Philadelphia, had no windows on its end walls, one of which faced a scenic south. But on the Potts house, that broad south wall, devoid of entrances for light and air, might have given pause to even a most dauntless purist.

The impure solution was partitions which ran to the face of the paneling, leaving the recesses between the chimneys as tiny ante-chambers. The dissonance between internal logic and exterior aesthetics was resolved; the axial arrangement of first story carriage door and second story window relieved an otherwise forbidding austerity on the south wall, and in the most eye-appealing way. It all may seem a bit awkward from a modern architect's viewpoint, but a highly dysfunctional and uncomfortable situation was averted.

JOINERY

Whether a house of the mid to late 18th century was constructed of wood, brick, or stone, a striking feature to the modern observer is the massive amount of finished woodwork, or "joinery." Workers in wood fell into two general classes, carpenters and joiners. Carpenters did the structural tasks, framing floors, walls, and rafters. Joiners did the refined finishing work, doors, windows, shutters, cornices, and paneling. A joiner's responsibility was primarily, but not exclusively, interior and by far the most demanding in terms of skill, time, and patience. The large mansions of the time had the most elaborate joinery, but even the smallest "proper" homes of merchants and gentlemen tradesmen were but scaled-down versions of the mansions. The Potts house is an excellent case-in-point.

Comparing the contours of ornamental moldings in Pennsylvania with contemporary work in New England or Virginia demonstrates that the joiners of that generation were schooled in the same texts. Every joiner and his assistants carried from job to job a collection of special molding planes. The woodwork profiles in Washington's headquarters incorporate larger and smaller ogees, ovolos, and quirked or double quirked beading.

These figures were building blocks of the classical style, that is, architectural patterns derived from the ancient precedents of Greece and Rome. What was not simply passed on from craftsman to craftsman could be found in manuals on ornamentation published in England, which were in turn based on adaptations of classical models by Renaissance architects like Vitruvius and Palladio. The south gable of the Potts house is a classic pediment. On a more specific scale, the cornices surrounding the main house at the roof eaves are textbook cases of the classical idiom. They are boxes; above the fascia is a double ogee, or *cyma recta* and *cyma reversa*. An ogee is a shape of a molding which makes an inward curve in the upper part and reverses itself into an outward curve on the lower part of the face of the molding, a so-called S-curve. The ogee normally is a horizontal molding. The soffit is joined to the wall by a molding combining ovolo and a cove. A cove is a strip with an inward curving slot. The cornice atop the paneling in the parlor is a smaller copy of the roof cornice.

Photograph of cornice

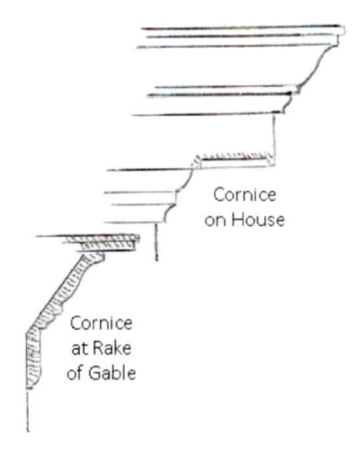

Drawing of a cornice

Whether combined into pure classical configurations or not, the basic moldings earlier described were used on all the decorative levels. Double ogees without the full cornice sit atop the paneling in the dining room and two bedrooms. Ogees and double quirked beading are found on the faces of exterior door frames, on trim around interior doors, window reveals, and on paneling trim surrounding fireplaces. Window frame faces combine the beading with ovolos.

Double quirked bead

Decorative levels followed a very definite order, or degree. The first floor front room was the parlor, the "best foot," so its decoration was the most elaborate. The trim around the doors and around the fully paneled window reveals were a combination of a large outer ogee, a smaller inner one, and a double quirked bead. This trim style is carried into the hallway as well, for this was, after all, the reception hall. The back room and the bedrooms were not so "public," so their trim was less complex. Door trim was simply the large ogee and the bead. Window reveals were not paneled; in the dining room they were plastered with only an ovolo inner corner strip. The bedroom reveals were plain boards with an ovolo inner edge.

Perhaps the most challenging and tedious work that an 18th century joiner confronted were stairways and window sash. The stairways of the Potts house are wholly open, from the first to the second floor, and from the second to the attic. In style, they are typical of the midcentury with their closed strings (the outer ends of the steps being covered). The area beneath the stairway from the first floor is encased by raised paneling and a paneled door leading to a steep basement stair. The underside of the landing (above the rear door) and of the stairs above the landing are lathed and plastered. The balustrades (end, or newel, posts) and balusters (pickets) of the railings are gracefully turned, doubtless on a lathe operated with a foot treadle.

Window design and construction also followed the conventions of the midcentury. The blown glass panes of the time were necessarily of small size, and those in the Potts house are close to the 8 by 10 inch dimension throughout. To have windows of any size, such as the twelve-over-twelve in the parlor or the eight-over-twelve on the upstairs façade, required sash with elaborate grids of dividers (muntins). In these guillotine windows, the upper sash was stationary, the lower slid up and down without supports or counterweights. There was no dividing strip between upper and lower sash. The outer face of the lower rubbed against the inner surface of the upper. As characteristic of the period, the sashes are barely over an inch thick, but the muntins are quite wide, about 1¼ inches in breadth. The stiles, rails and muntins are rabbetted on their outer edges to receive the glass; the inner edges are embellished with ovolos.

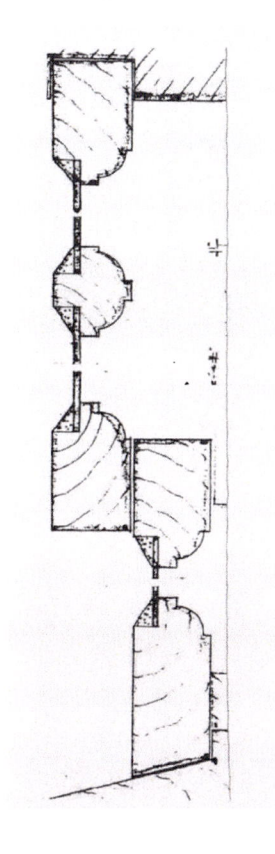

Devoid of storm windows, loose-fitting, and innocent of weather stripping, the windows were awesomely drafty. However, with open hearth heating, this was a practical necessity. A roaring open fire is insatiable for oxygen, so without a generous gale from around windows and doors, the fires would quickly have sputtered out. Fireplaces of the time did not as a rule have dampers with which to control the wasteful updraft. Comfortable seating during cold weather would have entailed delicate adjustments in order to avoid all the icy drafts. Some warmth during the night would have been retained by the downstairs solid shutters.

Drawing of window sash

A less conspicuous but absolutely basic phase of joinery was preparation of the flooring. The wide plank flooring was installed even before the inner partitions and certainly before the remaining joinery. Flooring of the time was very often yellow pine, as at Mount Vernon and the Potts house. The planks were rough sawn and then brought to size and smoothed by laborious application of scrub planes. In the Potts house they are tongue-and-groove, made so by use of so-called match planes. Wood shrinks as it seasons, so the narrowest floor boards were used on the first floor, the widest in the kitchen and attic where larger cracks between planks would be less offensive. Typical of the time, no finish of any kind was used.

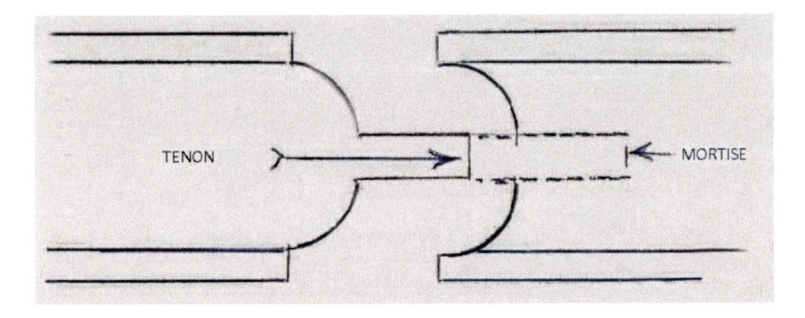

Drawing of mortise and tenon joint

Far and away the most exacting, laborious, and tedious part of 18th century joinery was joining of stiles, rails, and muntins in the doors, paneling, and windows. Every intersection required a mortise and tenon. The craftsmen of the time doubtless contrived many jigs and guides which simultaneously reduced the time and improved the precision, but they were naturally bound by hand tools. Every tenon had to be sawn; every mortise entailed a series of bored holes, followed by squaring the mortise with a chisel. Door and window joints were then secured by pegs, usually small, square tenons fitting into small, square mortises. The Potts house, small in size but rich in woodwork, demanded hundreds of such joints.

PANELING

Exterior view of window and shutters

The raised paneling used in the interior and exterior doors, the window reveals as earlier described, the outside window shutters, and the paneling which covers the fireplace walls in the four main rooms, is consistent throughout the house and typical of the time.

The panels are about ¾ inch thick with a feathered edge. The pieces which frame the panels, the stiles (vertical) and rails (horizontal) are about an inch thick, edged with a rabbet into which the panel fits and an ovolo on the face. As also consistent with the period, the raised face of the panel is flush with the face of the frame members.

On the exterior doors, the panels naturally face outward. The inner side of the doors is covered with thin vertical planks which add reinforcement and some insulation. These are attached with many hand-forged nails.

The window shutters are identically constructed, with the panels visible when the shutters are open. Interior doors lack the plank backing; their raised panels face the hall, the room side showing only flat, unornamented backsides of the panels and frames. Here again was a sort of propriety, as the hall was public.

When the rooms were "open," the doors would also be, revealing only the paneled faces. The rule is proved by an exception to this arrangement, the door to the parlor. This door is thicker and has the raised faces on both faces, entirely correct for the most formal, public chamber.

The glory of the house is without doubt the fully paneled fireplace walls of the main rooms. The parlor is appropriately the most handsome room, having the ornate cornice and door/fireplace trim described above. The fireplace has a fine marble facing.

The most elegant touches to the parlor are the arched tops on the doors to the cupboard and vestibule which flank the fireplace. The arches are broken at their summits by graceful key blocks, obviously modeled on classical precedents.

The paneling in the three other rooms is somewhat simpler; door tops are square and the fireplace surrounds are plastered.

Altogether, the paneling reflects the style of the midcentury.

Dining room – window, open cabinet

Second floor back bedroom - detail of paneling

While the house is now thought to have been built as late as 1774, such seeming period discrepancies were not especially significant in that day.

A puzzling feature of the front room (parlor) paneling is an obvious imbalance on the right side next to the window. The right jamb of the china cabinet encroaches nearly two inches onto the paneled window reveal. Symmetry would have dictated that the jamb edge merely touch the reveal or, more appropriately, be separated from it by two or more inches.

*Parlor paneling
detail of doorway to vestibule, moldings*

China cabinet (in red) in the parlor

The latter would have provided a true match to the vestibule door on the opposite side of the paneling. The raised paneling above the china cabinet could have been properly centered over the keyblock rather than askew. The joiner evidently tried to disguise the imbalance by making the raised panels equal in width. Alas, the stile dividing these panels is all too conspicuously offset from the keyblock. Why, then, this curiosity? Was it a miscalculation of the joiner which he was not required to correct? How could such an error have occurred? Might the paneling have been fabricated at another site according to inaccurate dimensions? Or could it all have been a deliberate whimsical dash of artistic license intending to leaven the severity of absolute symmetry? Could the craftsman, like a Greek artisan of old, have flawed an otherwise perfect creation in order to avert its demolition by jealous gods?

Close up of imbalance in paneling above china cabinet

Parlor paneling showing imbalance above china cabinet

Parlor paneling showing imbalance above china cabinet

    On the face of it, it was a major blunder of the joiner. But this conclusion is not easy to accept in view of the precision otherwise displayed in his workmanship. It is highly unlikely in that period that the paneling components would have been assembled elsewhere than on the job. In any case, it is hard to understand how such a blatant bungle would have been permitted to stand. That is, again, if it was a bungle. If it was deliberate, an artistic flare or personal statement by an anonymous prima donna of the molding plane, aesthetic judgments as to whether the contrivance "worked" may well vary. On this, as on so many other questions pertaining to historic structures, the field of speculation, debate, and judgment may remain open, conceivably forever.

The richness of the paneling is further dramatized by the extreme plainness of the remaining walls and ceilings in each room. It is unadorned plaster throughout, with no moldings at the confluence of walls and ceilings. Two binding threads, a chair rail and baseboard, run horizontally throughout both floors of the house, hallways included. On the first floor these relieve the severe verticality induced by the nine-foot ceilings, tall window openings, and small dimensions of the rooms. On the second floor, with a lower ceiling and no window seats, a much more horizontal aspect is found. A decorative detail peculiar to the Philadelphia region was painting the baseboard black, and then carrying the black strip unbroken across door bottoms and panelings at the same height as the baseboard. This has been reproduced in the present décor of the house.

This is an appropriate point to note a construction procedure common to that time but not done today. All of the interior finished woodwork, the joinery, was completed before the walls were plastered. This is astonishing in light of the great quantities of moisture involved in plaster work. Surely the raw woodwork absorbed dampness, tending thereby to swell and, to some extent, warp. It is possible that the woodwork was then primed prior to plastering in order to reduce its permeability. Whatever the case, the 18th century procedure was in at least one respect eminently reasonable. As a malleable medium, plaster could be easily applied to conform to any contour of the woodwork, forming an unbroken seal. The reverse is not true. Wood is not so malleable, so fitting it to the inevitable surface irregularities of dry plasterwork is practically impossible. Gaps are inevitable. A quick examination around door and window casings of a 20th century house will make this evident.

STRUCTURAL DETAILS

Mortises and tenons also figured in the rougher framing work. The floor joists between the first and second and second and third floors parallel the long dimension of the house. Their outer ends are set into the stonework, but the inner ends are mortised into a massive "summer" beam which runs north and south. The beam is the same height as the joists, about 7 ½ inches, so it is not visible, but its width is at least a foot. These beams were exposed in houses of the earlier colonial period, but the more refined taste of the mid 18th century required that such rudimentary structural details be concealed.

Despite the massiveness of the summers, they would not have supported their burdens without pronounced sagging except for reinforcement from the partitions. The partitions between the front and back rooms fall directly beneath the beams, and the "T" at which these intersect with the partitions between the rooms and hallways would be the points of greatest strength. The partitions are a solid two inches thick, formed of vertical one inch planks, overlapping and nailed together.

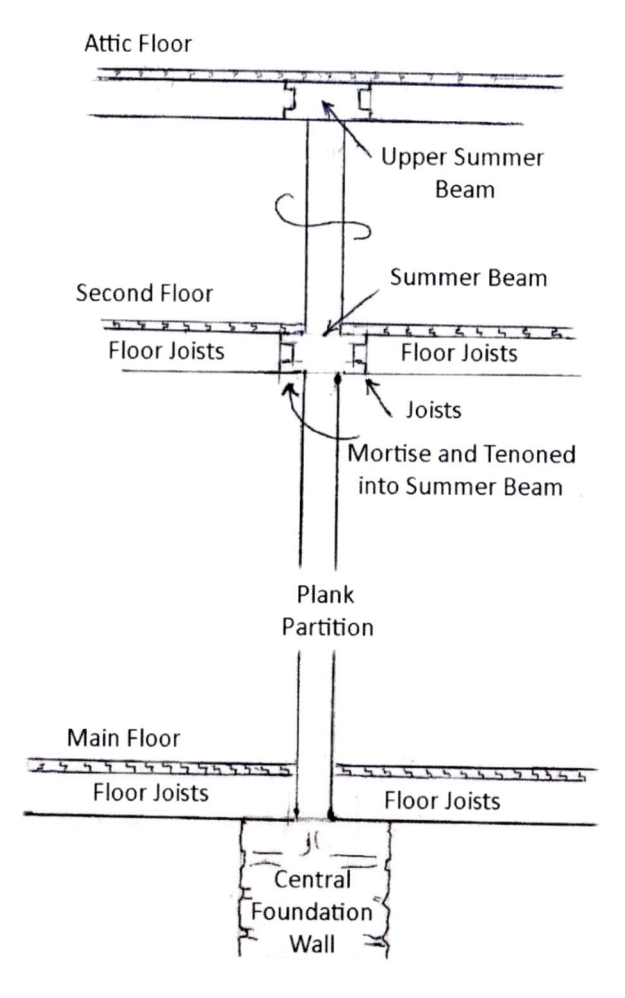

Drawing of detail of floor structure

Plasterwork is held to the partitions by hand-split wood lath which is nailed directly to the planks with hand-forged nails. This method is used even on the back of the paneling in the first floor south vestibule and the second floor window closet. There was no room behind the lath for the "keys," which is plaster that slops over the back of the lath and keys it on. But the hand-split lath was evidently rough enough on its edges to support plaster on a vertical surface. A ceiling would be a different story, but in this case there is space behind the lath for the keys. Plaster's strength was greatly enhanced by a stringiness provided by ample quantities of horsehair. On the exterior walls, plaster is applied directly to the stone without lath.

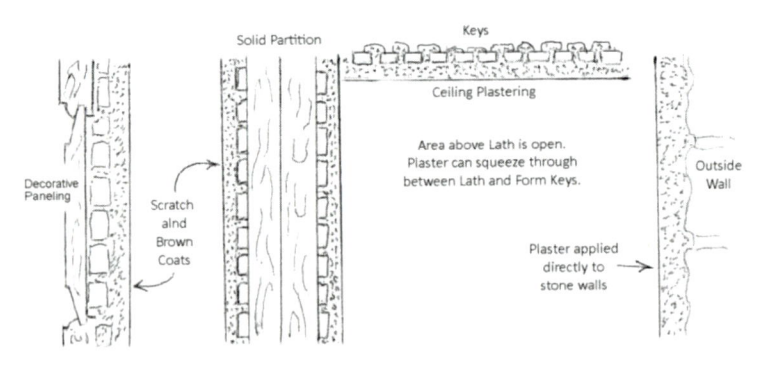

Drawing of plasterwork (cutaway view)

Plaster was multi-layered, the first, or "scratch" coat, being a mixture of gypsum and an aggregate like sand, bound together with horse hairs. It was the coat which bound the plaster directly to lath or stone. The second coat was much like the first but with less horsehair. This "brown" coat, coarse and gritty in texture, was probably so called because it was brownish in color when dry. Normally, the final coat was without aggregate, consisting of slaked lime and a hardener. It gave a smooth, hard surface to the wall. It is now believed that the Potts house did not at first have a finished coat, the brown coat being covered with perhaps a paper and paint concoction called "distemper."[2] Thus it must have been applied when Washington occupied the dwelling, the finish lime coat not being applied until after the Revolution.

In the 18th century, plaster was nearly always whitewashed, being either dead white or off-white in tone. The woodwork was painted in peacock colors, deep Indian reds, vivid green, or blue tones, which contrasted vividly with walls and ceilings. This is not merely speculation. Samples of early paint have been uncovered, and the current reproductions represent the best that modern paint analysis can offer. More will be said on this later.

The foregoing description has sought to depict the Potts house as it was in its beginnings.

More will be said about the kitchen wing later. As stated earlier, the wing is more an object of speculation than of description, for so little remains of the original, at least above the foundations.

CHAPTER FOUR

OWNERSHIP-THE FIRST 100 YEARS

The years following the army's evacuation in 1778 are shrouded in historical mist. Immediately after the departure the landscape was a desolate quagmire: timber extensively cut back for fuel and huts; rutted paths and earthworks covering the terrain. Yet, an 18th-century army left little detritus that was "non-biodegradable." As in any pastoral setting of that time, physical surroundings quickly reassumed a familiar pattern. Crops were planted. Weeds consumed the latrines and trenches. Farmers plundered breastworks and huts for fencing and firewood. In the summer of 1787, during a recess of the Constitutional Convention, Chairman Washington rode out with Gouverneur Morris to fish for shad in the Schuylkill River. Washington left the fishing to Morris and used the time to tour the old grounds. He had to strain his imagination to recall the scene of a decade earlier. Crops obliterated the encampment lanes, and fortifications were in ruins. Remnants of huts endured in wooded spots where plows had not cut. Washington did not mention his old headquarters house.[1]

To resurrect manufacturing near Valley Creek required considerably more effort than farming, but it was apparently accomplished with dispatch. The continuing war meant intense demand for ironware. The property of Colonel William Dewees and David Potts had suffered greatly by the British depredations and the decimation of their woodlands by the Continental army during the encampment. However, their prewar partnership continued, and they set about immediately to construct a new forge. A so-called tilt mill was erected downstream from the pre-revolutionary forge, that is, closer to the old mill dam from which the race to the saw mill and grist mill took off. On the west side of Valley Creek, in Chester County, slitting and rolling mills were also constructed. Dewees was man on the spot, supervising construction and serving as ironmaster for many years; David Potts remained in Philadelphia, marketing wares produced at the forge.[2] By 1780, David's son James was ready to take over the Philadelphia outlet, permitting his father to move to the valley.[3] David's presence may have been urgent because of the financial disaster which befell Dewees, perhaps in that year.

  The failure of William Dewees made Isaac sole partner with his brother, David, in the iron works. Dewees went bankrupt, perhaps as an effect of British vandalism (his son fought vainly for years to get compensation from the United States for his father's losses in the patriot cause). Personal misfortune, mismanagement, or even the extravagance attributed to him by the historian Henry Woodman could have intensified his plight. His assets were liquidated by sheriff's sale, terminating his connection with the family.[4] His property may in part or whole have been bought by the Potts brothers. The legal confusion caused by the departure of Dewees induced David and Isaac to separate their own properties into clearly delineated tracts.

Isaac Potts' role in local activity at this time is not known. Quaker meeting house records indicate that he did not transfer membership back from the Exeter meeting until 1782. However, he must have participated in reconstruction of the forges. The grist mill and saw mill, which were not attacked by the British, continued under his management as before. While Isaac's residence remained Pottsgrove, he may have resided periodically at Valley Forge before 1782.

For lack of evidence to the contrary, one may assume that Isaac and his family finally resided in his house on a regular basis for a few years after 1782. He was now active in management of both the mills and the forges, the ironworks being called "Isaac Potts and Company" by 1786. David, who remained in Valley Forge until his death in 1798, lived in the L-shaped stone dwelling 600 feet south of Isaac's, just north of the Gulph Road and east of Valley Creek. This place was originally situated on the southern edge of Isaac's mill tract but was later, probably sometime after the encampment, legally relocated to the forge tract south of the Gulph Road. It thus became David Pott's domicile. A structure had existed for many years on the site, predating even the ownership of John Potts, the father of

Isaac, but David remodeled and modernized it during this period.[5]

Isaac's ambitions were soon to uproot him. In 1784, he held title to 105 acres of land, his original mill tract plus, in all probability, tracts contiguous or in close proximity to it. In December, 1784, he sold half of his holdings, a segment which by 1787 was in the hands of one Norris Jones. By 1790, Jones was dead and the stage was set for this notice in the Pennsylvania Gazette:

TO BE SOLD BY PUBLIC VENDUE,

On Seventh Day, the 6th of next month, at the Merchants' Coffee-house, in the city of Philadelphia, at 6 o'clock in the evening,

THE GREAT VALLEY WORKS ESTATE

No. 1. A forceable forge, with four fires and two hammers, well founded on a large dam of 17 feet head and fall. Also an excellent slitting and rolling mill upon the same dam, with a large stone coal house to each. Also a good stone house and barn, blacksmith and cooper's shop, with a number of small houses to accommodate workmen. With these will be sold about 650 acres of land, of which about 15 acres of watered meadow, 550 ditto plow land, the remainder woodland, part of which has been cut many years, and is now in a thriving state.

No.2. A capital grist mill and saw mill, worked by the above stream. The grist mill has two water wheels, three pair of stones and two sets of bolting works. On the premises are a good stone house, kitchen stabling, about seven acres of meadow, 30 plow land and 40 woodland. The situation of the above described works being on the banks of the Schuylkill, about 20 miles from Philadelphia, and on the road leading from the forges and furnaces, in the interior parts of this state, to Philadelphia, being also drove by the Valley Creek. Which is now known to be a superior stream, chiefly fed by springs, and therefore not liable to dry in summer nor freeze in winter, render them peculiarly advantageous in carrying on the various branches of business.

No. 3. A farm, containing 200 acres. On this tract are a good log dwelling house, with a good spring near the door, a small orchard, about 10 acres of watered meadow, and 15 more may be made at a small expence, as part thereof is cleared and ditched, about 40 acres of plow land, the remainder is woodland, part of which has been cut, and is now in a thriving state.

No. 4. A farm, containing 100 acres, has a good house, a small orchard and a meadow, about 40 acres of cleared land, and the remainder in woods.

No. 5. A farm, containing 230 acres, or thereabouts. On this tract are a large log dwelling house and a good spring near the door, an orchard, about 100 acres clear, the remainder timbered. The quality strong land, and may, with improvement, be made an excellent farm, being contiguous to Limestone.

For terms apply to Isaac Potts, on the premises; Isaac Lloyd, of Darby; or Thomas Harrison, in Philadelphia.

Should the above premises not be sold by private sale before the time above fixed, attendance will be given at the time and place of sale by Isaac Potts,

    ISAAC LLOYD and   Executors to the estate

    THOMAS HARRISON,   of Norris Jones, dec.

Philadelphia, 10 month 11, 1790.

Items No. 1 and 2 were apparently the remaining Potts family holdings in the Valley, David's and Isaac's. The remainder was from the Norris Jones estate, including the parcel already purchased from Isaac. Isaac was acting as agent for his brother as well as himself. What David's plans were is unknown, but he continued to live on the premises until his death eight years later. Isaac was disposing of his estate to raise capital for a new venture elsewhere. In the early 1790s he moved to Philadelphia prior to building an iron works (Martha Furnace, in honor of his wife) across the Delaware River in New Jersey. Isaac was its ironmaster from first blast in 1793.[6]

If the auction took place, its results are not known. Only in December, 1793, did Isaac sell the other half of his property to Jacob Paul of Germantown, the husband of Mary Bolton, sister of Isaac's wife, Martha. In April, 1795, Paul acquired the other half from the Jones estate. The 105 acre segment, which included the headquarters house, was again intact. With Jacob's death in 1806, his son Joseph Paul inherited the property and held it until 1826. As for the ironworks, David apparently continued to own them until his death. By then he had sold off a considerable portion of the woodland he and Dewees had purchased years earlier. He nevertheless passed on 800 acres, mostly woodland, to his son James and a son-in-law who then ran the forge, slitting and rolling mills.[7]

The advertisement mentioned two good stone houses. That in conjunction with the forges (item No.1) may have been David Potts' house. There is no proof of this, but the inclusion of a barn strengthens the case. However, the reference may have been to a stone house east of the lower dam (now disappeared) or even to the Dewees house, about 300 yards west of the stream, south of the Gulph Road. In No. 2 in the advertisement, compare the "good stone house, kitchen and stabling" with the description in the rental offering of 1776. It is possible to quibble with the identity of the house in the 1776 notice, but the 1790 structure is confirmed by association with the grist and saw mills. In both advertisements, the kitchen is described in terms that hint a semi-detached dependency or wing, concurring with what is now believed to have been the configuration at that time. From a modern perspective, it is striking to find in the 1790 notice no mention of the Potts house's historic role or even the encampment in general. Heroic associations with the American Revolution were not yet recognized as marketable enhancements to a property.

The first known legal description of the house appears in a federal tax record of 1798.[8] The United States was in an undeclared naval war with France, and many in John Adams' administration anticipated an imminent full scale conflict. A crash program to build up a navy was underway, but money was desperately needed. The administration floated a direct tax on property proportioned to the estimated wealth and population of the various states. The initial measure assessed not only the value of land and primary structures but even counted outbuildings and window panes in houses. This hearkened back, possibly, to an old English practice of taxing houses by the number of windows. The program provoked such a hostile reaction that it was abandoned. Nevertheless, a direct tax was highly unpopular and weakened Adams and his Federalist party on the eve of the general election of 1800.

But a notoriously impolitic tax program proved a blessing for architectural historians, for it recorded physical details of early houses otherwise unknowable. Consider the descriptions of the headquarters house and David Potts' house. The headquarters was owned by Jacob Paul and evidently being rented out once again. The dimensions of both the main house and kitchen wing are approximately correct, assuming that the dogtrot is included in the kitchen measurements. Especially significant is that the kitchen is only one story in height. The measurements of David Potts' house also coincide with its modern size.

1798 FEDERAL DIRECT TAX					
Description	Washington HQ		David Potts' house		
	House	Kitchen	House	Kitchen	Ice House
Occupant	Richard Rudd		David Potts		
Dwelling	1		1		
Appurtenance		1		1	1
Dimensions	27x30	16x24	21x66	18x27	10x10
Material	Stone	Stone	Stone	Stone	Stone
# Stories	2	1	2		
Windows	8/3		10/19		
Lights	18/15		18/12		
Outhouses	1		2		
Land (Acres)	1		1		
Valuation	650		1450		

Federal Direct Tax, 1798 – Upper Merion "Window Pane Tax"[8]

The description of windows in the headquarters is puzzling. It does not coincide with the known number of windows nor with the number of lights. In the windows as known today, there are three with 24 lights and four with 20 lights each. However, in the dozen of houses enumerated, no windows had more than 18 lights. This may have been the maximum number counted. But in that event, the headquarters should have had nine windows with 18 lights. The original arrangement of the windows of the kitchen wing is questionable, but on the main house there are two windows with 15 lights. Not even mentioned are three windows with 12 lights each. Not knowing the criteria of the assessors, one is hard put to make sense of the records. Further research may shed light on this question. The possibility of simple carelessness on the part of the assessors cannot be discounted.

Before leaving the early period of the house's history, a brief digression on the human dimension is appropriate. What do we know about Isaac Potts? An interest in his home naturally leads to an interest in its original owner. But the dense cloud of time is a formidable barrier to resurrecting his personality. Much is known of the outline of his life but almost nothing of the man. As with most people of history, no letter, diaries, or other personal records are known to have survived. That leaves only meeting house records, deeds and other legal documents, and the family history by Mrs. Potts James with its invaluable collection of information, both solid and apocryphal. There is little beyond this but inference.

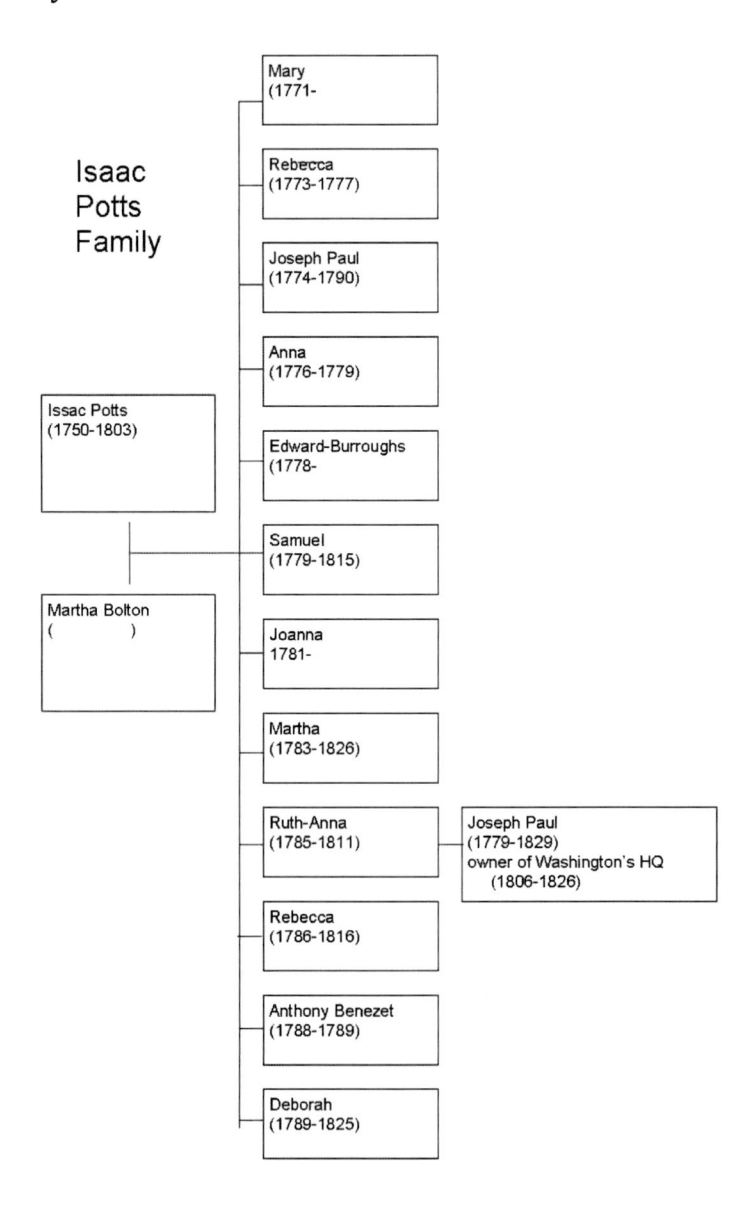

Isaac Potts Family

- **Isaac Potts (1750-1803)** + **Martha Bolton ( )**
  - Mary (1771-
  - Rebecca (1773-1777)
  - Joseph Paul (1774-1790)
  - Anna (1776-1779)
  - Edward-Burroughs (1778-
  - Samuel (1779-1815)
  - Joanna 1781-
  - Martha (1783-1826)
  - Ruth-Anna (1785-1811)
    - Joseph Paul (1779-1829) owner of Washington's HQ (1806-1826)
  - Rebecca (1786-1816)
  - Anthony Benezet (1788-1789)
  - Deborah (1789-1825)

Historical evidence indicates that Isaac Potts was moderately well-to-do. From his accomplishments one can infer that he was a hardheaded and ambitious businessman. There is little to set him apart from many dozen contemporary entrepreneurs in Pennsylvania alone. He begat a total of 12 children, eight of whom survived him. Such mortality was unremarkable for the age.

He and his wife were Quakers and probably devout as suggested by the following quotation from his will:

> Life is uncertain, I am in a poor state of health and am to set out on a journey tomorrow, which consideration must apologize to my friends and the public for this unmethodical will: but I feel easiest to leave it as it is, with a mind clothed (I think) with the spring and glow of universal love to my fellow creatures not doubting but the true members the world over of the one true Church Militant will meet again in the Church triumphant. Amen. Farewell.[9]

Potts' spiritual convictions may have colored his attitude toward slavery. He was from a significant slave holding family and shared some slaves bequeathed by his father's estate. Still, a son born in 1788 was named after a famous Quaker, Anthony Benezet, best remembered as a foe of slavery. The 1790 census showed no slaves in Isaac's household.[10] His slaves may thus have been by the late 1780s disposed of by death, manumission, or sale.

Mrs. Potts James is the only known source for a glimpse of the person behind the name. In her words, Isaac was a man of "infinite jest and humor," but she did not reveal how she knew this. Her quotation from a Quaker obituary, appearing in a Philadelphia newspaper of June, 1803, is probably the only surviving commentary on Potts from his time. One line is particularly suggestive: "His unreserved candor rendered him obnoxious to many unjust censures, which have been too frequently pronounced against him with underserved acrimony."[11]

Obituaries are rarely reliable portraits of the departed whom they often elevate to patently false saintliness. It is essential to read between the lines. Was the real Isaac Potts a forthright, honest man, devout but with a droll sense of humor? Or did the obituary put the best face on what needed to be disguised? Did he make his enemies honestly through tactlessness, sarcasm, or ill-humor? The historical Isaac Potts will never be much more than a name, just another life lost forever in the shadows of a distant day.

A justified speculation on Potts and his family would be their living conditions during the ten years, more or less, after the encampment, when they are thought to have occupied the Valley Forge house. It is wholly conjectural but warranted by general knowledge of society in that time. Appropriate to their means and social status, the family would have had at least two full-time servants, perhaps a cook and housekeeper. In that small house, the servants would have been sheltered in the garret or the half story above the kitchen. If the 1790 census is accurate, there were four free white males over 16 years old in the household who were not part of the immediate family. They might have included an apprentice or two, a dependent relative or two, but there would also doubtless have been one or two live-in servants. Mill hands and forge laborers would render additional service in cutting firewood for the house, repairs and painting, landscape maintenance, care of horses, carriage, etc. Obviously, the Potts family did not live in the lavish style of a Tidewater planter or a Philadelphia mercantile grandee, but one proper for a comfortable entrepreneurial household of the period.

The Potts family name passed from the scene shortly after 1800, but the valley continued to attract various manufacturers who utilized the force of the stream. The old ironworks were carried on by a series of owners, but not many found their businesses very lucrative. By 1814, two partners set up a hardware manufacturing business, but the end of the War of 1812 found the nation glutted with English made goods whose prices could not be met by the relatively primitive American factories. The depressed condition of United States manufacturers in these years was reflected in the economy of the valley.

Conditions improved by the early 1820s. A Philadelphia entrepreneur leased land on the west side of the Valley Creek (Chester County) to set up an armory for making weapons under a federal contract. In 1821, a cotton factory was located on the site of the iron forge built by Dewees, Isaac and David Potts right after the encampment, immediately south of the Gulph Road and east of the Valley Creek. Many new houses and utility buildings were erected during these years, so the compact manufacturing hamlet of the Revolutionary era had swollen into a true mill town.[12]

The mid 1820s witnessed a curious experiment in "alternative life styles." The communitarian theories of Robert Owen of New Lanark, an English humanitarian industrialist, were introduced to America in 1825. The purest application of Owen's idea was New Harmony on the Wabash River in Indiana, but American susceptibility to utopian cults knew few bounds in that time. Nine other "Owenite" communities were set up in the States, one of which was Valley Forge. Owen believed man's nature to be totally malleable, and if he were in a humane, cooperative, non-exploitative environment, his personality would take on those qualities. He would be benign, non-competitive, and thoroughly virtuous. Owen called for company towns based on profit-sharing, gender equality, and cradle-to-grave security. An army of idealists flocked into these noble experiments, investing money, time, and incalculable emotional energy.

In 1826, about three hundred of the faithful descended on Valley Forge and set up the "Friendly Association for Mutual Interests." Modeled on Owen's precepts, the association's constitution included women in the directorship. All members of the company town would be "Moral, Sober and Industrious," freely contributing to the useful work necessary to make the business enterprise a success. Women were "equally to enjoy the pleasures of social intercourse and the acquisition of knowledge."[13] The group purchased a number of buildings in the settlement, including Washington's headquarters which became the "capitol."[14]

Therefore, the headquarters finally passed from the Paul family which had owned it since 1793, severing the last familial link with Isaac Potts. In early 1826, Joseph Paul deeded 114 acres, which included the mills, to a Joseph Thomas, who in turn deeded the same property in August to James Jones, one of the wealthier members of the Harmonist experiment.[15]

By the next year, the experiment had collapsed, torn apart like all the other Owenite communities by dissension and withdrawal of disenchanted investors. However, Jones retained the house which remained in his family for the next half century.

THE FATE OF THE WING

Current scholarly surmise is that it was James Jones, with a family of five children, who found the house too cramped and had the kitchen wing enclosed and enlarged. The original wing is now supposed to have been one to one-and-a-half stories in height and semi-detached, joined to the house by a breezeway with an arched opening at the front. This was replaced by a wing two full stories in height with the dogtrot eliminated, the opening filled in, except for a door, and the kitchen extended the full length of the wing. No primary documentation exists of this remodeling, but it is now believed that Jones carried it out in the late 1820s, soon after he acquired the house.[16] In about 1837, the Joneses dug a root cellar, or milk cave, at the north end of the wing, setting the stage for the relentless myth that a "secret passage" to the river had been dug for the possible escape of General Washington. As will be seen, both the wing reconstruction and the root cellar spawned mysteries to bedevil later generations.

With the American Revolution fading into the glow of a more distant past and a growing fascination with the young nation's first great epic, artifacts and places of the Revolution were getting increased attention from historians, patriots, and the public. Valley Forge was little honored by the revolutionary generation. Isaac Potts' notice of 1790 made no mention of the locality's or the house's historical significance. But by the 1830s and '40s, Valley Forge was taking on its own special aura, symbolizing deep despair, suffering, but also steadfast courage and triumph over insuperable odds. In short, as the years went by the snows of 1777-1778 got deeper and the temperatures colder, the indomitable spirit of Washington and his soldiers provided perfect fodder for romantic nationalism. Scenes of ragged soldiers huddling by their fires and Washington praying in the snow became as familiar as the flag and the Declaration of Independence.

Engraving showing one-story log cabin wing, 1840

During the 1840s, published drawings and engravings of the headquarters house began to appear. The invitation to a centennial celebration in 1877 of the army's evacuation carried a picture on its cover, ostensibly from an 1840 engraving, showing the house with a one-story log cabin wing.

This depiction, puzzling in itself, is thrown into further question by its discrepancy with other drawings of the house made in nearly the same period. Sherman Day, in his 1843 "Historical Collections of the State of Pennsylvania," showed a full two-story wing, perhaps of stone, covered with whitewash or even plaster.[17]

Engraving - full two-story wing by Sherman Day, 1843

Benson Lossing produced a diminutive sketch which agreed essentially with that by Day.[18]

Sketch of Headquarters by Benson Lossing, 1852

The drawings in both works were taken from nearly the same angle. The main body of the house appears much as it does today, but both drawings show the substantial two-story wing, nearly windowless and quite discordant with the architecture of the main house, with a doorway in front. Why, then, the log cabin in the 1840 drawing?

The clues lie in textual commentaries by both Day and Lossing. Lossing pointed out that

> *"this view was from the Reading rail-road looking east, and included a portion of the range of hills in the rear whereon the Americans were encamped. The main building was erected in 1770; the wing is more modern, and occupies the place of the log addition mentioned by Mrs. Washington in a letter to Mercy Warren, written in March, 1778."*[19]

Before quoting Lossing's letter, Day noted: "The wing is of modern structure, but it occupies the site of a smaller wing that was erected for the accommodation of Mrs. Washington."[20]

Erroneousness aside, Day's comment was also historically absurd. As was clear from Martha's own letter, the log cabin was not erected for her convenience. Wherever the structure to which she referred was located, it was built to accommodate the staff, officers, and frequent guests who often dined with George and Martha Washington.

But here lies the key to the conventional wisdom of the 1840s (and long after) as far as the kitchen wing was concerned. Observers of the time could see that the wing was not of the same age or formal style as the main section. They then jumped to the conclusion that Lady Washington's log cabin had been the predecessor to the relatively rustic "modern" wing. Hence, whoever produced the 1840 engraving was not recording what was there but how he imagined the log addition might have looked. The observers implicitly assumed that the house was without an attached kitchen wing before the encampment. Obviously, they were all aware of Martha's log cabin letter but not of Isaac Potts' advertisement of 1776, mentioning "a kitchen adjoining," nor of the 1798 glass tax which listed a stone wing. The mischief of Martha's letter had only begun.

The earliest photographic views of the headquarters arrived 20 years later. An 1859 stereopticon print gives an ill defined view of it from the south, taken from above the Gulph Road very near its crossing over the Valley Creek. This photograph has the virtue of showing the general environs, nearby buildings of the period, as well as flooding of the Valley Creek bed, presumably by a dam near the stream's mouth.

The first known photograph to focus on the house itself is from 1861. The house looks substantially as it did in Day's and Lossing's drawings, except for the annex behind the wing, just visible over the sloping roof of the shed. The annex was perhaps added in the years between the drawings and the photograph. From about this period are some of the photos taken from the southwest, exposing the opposite end of the house.

The sketches of Lossing, Day and Mrs. Potts James show alterations in the original form of the house which were undoubtedly done earlier in the 19th century. The sketch in Mrs. Potts James book shows that the oculus sash in the south gable had been taken out, the circular space filled in around a rectangular sash. This may have been done for ventilation but certainly not for aesthetics. The pent eave on the south gable is intact, but on the north end, as shown in the photograph of 1861, it had clearly been removed to make way for the roof of the raised wing.

1859 stereopticon print – Headquarters in background

First known photograph of house taken 1861 by Lewis Horning

Sketch of residence of Isaac Potts in Mrs. Potts James Memorial Book (pre 1874)

The photos as well as the sketches also reveal the altered physical environs of the house. Both Day and Lossing noted that their drawings were made from the roadbed of the Reading Railroad. The 1861 photograph was almost certainly made from there as well. During the 1830s, the railroad was constructed along the river bank on an elevated roadbed, creating a devastating and permanent intrusion upon the surroundings of the headquarters. The view of the river which the house had always enjoyed was obliterated forever. The 1760 grist mill of Isaac Potts yielded to progress as well. In 1843, a locomotive spark set fire to it and destroyed it.[21]

In his classic work on the Revolutionary War, Lossing gives the first glimpse of the Potts house interior since the encampment. On a visit which he dated November, 1848, he was received by James Jones and his wife.

> *He was quite feeble; but his wife, a cheerful old lady of nearly the same age, was the reverse, and, with vigorous step, proceeded to show us the interior of the building. Washington's room was small indeed. In the deep east window, whence he could look out upon a large portion of his camp upon the neighboring slopes, are still preserved the cavity and little trapdoor, arranged by the Commander-in-Chief as a private depository for his papers. It answered the purpose admirably; for even now the visitor would not suspect that the old blue sill upon which he was leaning to gaze upon the hallowed hills, might be lifted and disclose a capacious chest.[22]*

A troubling discrepancy plagues Lossing's account. If his visit was indeed in November, 1848, the feeble old man could hardly have been James Jones who died in 1842. The visit must have been much earlier than the date noted.

But the details on the house are interesting. The room shown to him as Washington's (first floor, east) is still so identified. Whether correct or not, the tradition goes back a long way as does the belief that the "old blue sill" of the window seat disguised a compartment especially created for Washington to hide his papers. There really is a concealed compartment under a removable window seat, but there is nothing to prove that it was custom made for Washington, even though he may well have used it. Lossing also notes that: "Near the headquarters of Washington were the ruins of an old flour-mill, whose clack was heard before the Revolution, nor ceased until within a few years."[23]

Unfortunately, "ruins" does not define whether the mill had burned down or simply deteriorated. As it was reputedly destroyed by fire in 1843, more precision would have helped to fix the date of his visit.

In his will of February 27, 1842, James Jones left the house to his wife, Ann, and the remainder of his estate to sons Nathan, Caleb, and John, and daughters Ann and Hannah. At his wife's death, the house would go to the daughters "while they are still alive and single."[24] In 1850, daughter Ann surrendered her half share in the house and two acres to her sister, Hannah Jones Ogden, who was already a widow.[25] The 1850 census listed the household as JONES, Ann, 70, Hannah Ogden, 41, Caleb P. Jones, 31 (wood agent for railroad), Ann Jones, 28, Lorenzo Sitzelberger, b. Germany, 35 (laborer). John and Nathan Jones were no longer beneath the parental roof by 1850.[26]

Widow Ogden occupied the headquarters house for at least the next 27 years. An unmarried brother, Caleb, who lived with her, was a freight agent for the Philadelphia and Reading Railroad. He was also a surveyor who, in 1840, mapped the area of the encampment, assisted by a man who had been a drummer with Washington's army in 1777-1778. Another brother, Nathan, built a stone house of Victorian design just south of the Potts house stable around 1870. (This stylistic anachronism was demolished in modern times). In her later years, Hannah reputedly ran a kindergarten in her home.

A lodger in the headquarters near the end of Mrs. Ogden's ownership threw some light on Washington's famous "secret passage" to the river. A young Methodist minister, Reverend William Powick, arrived in Valley Forge in March, 1879, and moved into the house as a boarder. While there he courted and married Hannah Ogden's niece, daughter of her sister Ann. As he carried butter and milk in and out of the cave, he became curious about the subterranean passageway, already a popular legend. In 1890, he wrote Hannah's older brother, Nathan, to ask about it. In his response, Nathan remembered being involved in digging the cave about 1840, but saw no sign of an underground tunnel. The earth around the digging was perfectly solid; had there been a surviving tunnel, he would surely have seen it.[27]

Even if this news had been universally broadcast, it probably would not have dissipated the myth. The cold light of facts rarely chases away edifying rumors or exciting legends. The story remained alive and well for at least the next half century.

The most memorable survival from Hannah Ogden was a comment on her residence in a letter to Mrs. Potts James, who visited Mrs. Ogden at the headquarters about 1870. Mrs. Potts James received a letter from her hostess describing the burning of the old grist mill. As for the headquarters Mrs. Ogden writes:

> *If the house is as old as the mill, it has stood the storms of over a century well. There are the same doors and window-shutters (as well as sash) as when the house was built, and it may last another generation if some progressive owner don't get it and despise its antiquity.*[28]

Through over a century of private ownership, the headquarters had, with the exception of the kitchen wing, managed to retain much of its original character. The fate of the wing is symptomatic of how easily the whole building could have been denatured under private ownership. Of course, the house was always known as Washington's Headquarters, and how much this may have deterred the altering hands of owners is impossible to gauge.

CHAPTER FIVE

PUBLIC OWNERSHIP & RESTORATION ACTIVIY

From the mid 19th century on, many patriotic organizations sprang up to honor and preserve the nation's past. Inspired by the Mount Vernon Ladies Association which solicited private subscriptions to acquire and restore Washington's home, the Centennial and Memorial Association of Valley Forge was set up in 1878 to prepare a celebration for the centennial of the encampment and to purchase and preserve the headquarters house. The group was headed by Mrs. Anna Morris Holstein, entitled Lady Regent. Among a host of Vice Regents was Mrs. Potts James. In March, 1878, an agreement was made with Mrs. Ogden to purchase her house for $6,000. Mrs. Ogden was no longer living in the house by this time.[1]

Anna Morris Holstein

The Association set the 19th of June for the extravaganza, one hundred years to the day after

Washington and his army evacuated. The well-publicized gathering featured the governor and other notables for long-winded oratory, picnics, prayers, and military ensembles for elaborate parade-ground pomp. An estimated crowd of 20,000 to 30,000 descended on the scene, most arriving by train.

For the first time in its history the headquarters house was open to a curious public. The mob was intimidating. Each visitor was charged ten cents to see the interior which was given mostly to exhibiting artifacts of the American Revolution, many of which were unrelated to Valley Forge. A few furniture items were represented as having been in the house when Washington was there, a more than dubious claim. Also,

> ... *in one of the ancient trees which surround the dwelling, a little hatchet was stuck, presumably the one with which George demolished the cherry tree. This, however, was not distinctly asserted.* [2]

Mrs. Holstein and her colleagues guided several thousand visitors through the house, selling stereoscopic prints and commemorative medals contributed by the United States mint. The behavior of souvenir hunters, especially on the outside, sounded a sour note:

> *A part of the day there were no soldiers to guard the property and keep away those of the crowd inclined to be*

troublesome. Corners of the building were broken off and carried away as mementoes.

The association enjoyed a return of $410 on the Day's activity at the headquarters, a down payment on its costly plans for the future.[2]

Cornerstone

One year later the Association committed a puzzling act which would be unthinkable among historical preservationists today. It invited the Free and Accepted Masons of the State of Pennsylvania to dedicate the headquarters building by the laying of a cornerstone. In the ceremony on the 19th of June, 1879, the new stone was inserted into a prepared notch on a corner of the building containing "documents, coins, and other valuable articles" in a box which was deposited in a cavity of the stone. The proceedings reveal that the cornerstone was placed "at the southeast angle of the building."³ The only stone now identifiable as such is at the southeast corner of the building, about five feet above the ground, machine-dressed and not matching the original walls. It shows clearly in the photograph of the cornerstone on the previous page.

A conscientious restorationist of today would use every means precisely to match the materials and methods congenial to an historic rehabilitation. A machine-dressed cornerstone into the Potts house would be unthinkable.

The real challenge to the Association was to secure funds with which to pay off the $6,000 mortgage. On the 1st of May, 1879, Hannah Ogden ceded 22 acres to William Holstein, Lady Regent's husband, for $6,000. On the following 4th of February, another acre, the one containing the headquarters, was transferred from Ogden to Holstein, also for $6,000.⁴ The meaning of the earlier transfer is unknown, for the latter one conveyed the headquarters parcel. Holstein was evidently serving as trustee. Meeting the mortgage proved an epic and very nearly futile struggle.

The national economy was in lean times; contributions dwindled to a trickle; nation-wide appeals brought disappointing response; fund-raising events produced meager results. A local chapter of a national organization, Patriotic Order Sons of America, came to the rescue, and only through its beneficence was the debt finally retired. On the 9th of November, 1886, William Holstein deeded the one acre containing the house to the Centennial and Memorial Association of Valley Forge.[5]

The financial rescue of the Association enabled it to gain clear title to the headquarters in 1886 and led to some additional financial windfalls. After exhausting work by a committee of the Association, a $5,000 grant was secured from the Pennsylvania State Legislature. Added contributions by the Patriotic Order Sons of America amounted to $1,400. With such a princely sum in its coffers, the Association was able to purchase a strip of land adjacent to the original headquarters parcel, to construct a caretaker's house near the headquarters, and carry out a major renovation and restoration of the headquarters.

Nathan Jones, owner of a sizable parcel of land behind (east of) the headquarters was approached with an offer of $400 per acre for some of his property, but he insisted on $800 per acre. The matter was deferred to a later date.

The Association, in its traditional meeting room, Washington's supposed office in the first floor rear room of the headquarters, pushed ahead with restoration plans. On the 18th of June, 1887, an architect was engaged for $100. By the 15th of July, the architect's plans were reviewed, and:

> *In the matter of improvements it was agreed that the stone annex should be torn down and a log cabin be erected in its place, to accord with the original condition*

of the premises in Washington's time. Mr. R.T.S. Hallowell, a member of the Board and a carpenter, was entrusted with the entire work of rejuvenation, restoration and new building ... The Committee having charge of improvements were empowered to draw upon the treasury to the amount of one thousand dollars without further consideration.[6]

Hallowell and his assistants worked fast; by the 18th of January, 1888, he reported the completion of work on the "old headquarters."

What was done is well recorded. On the main section, window frames and shutters were replaced as, possibly, were many window sashes. Some of the interior walls were re-plastered and the paneling was repainted. The rectangular three-light sash in the oculus of the south gable was replaced by a circular sash. The pent eave on the north gable, which had been removed to accommodate James Jones' raised wing, was replaced.

Most striking was the transformation of the wing. It was lowered from two to one-and-a-half stories, its floor level was lowered, and a breezeway fronted by a wide arch was inserted between the house and the kitchen. The kitchen floor joists had probably decayed, so they were replaced with concrete beams over which a modern wood floor was laid.

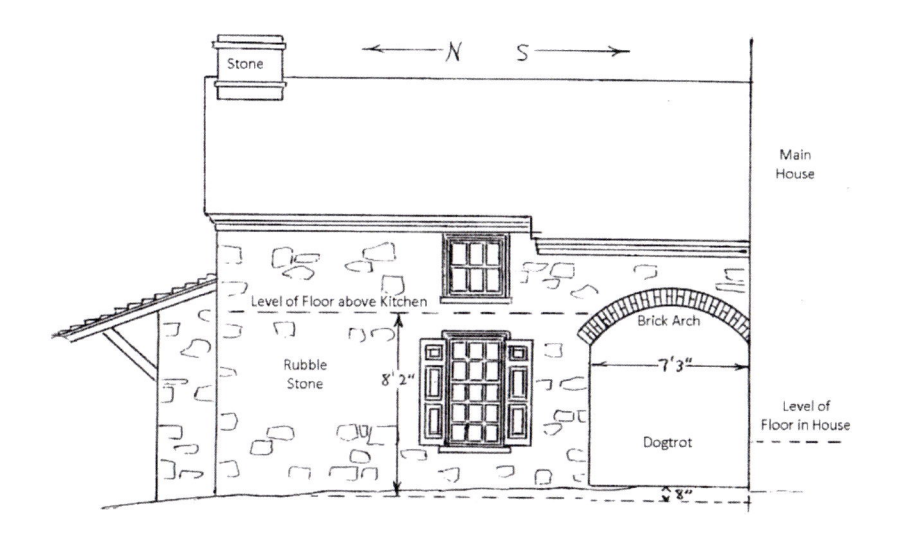

Drawing of 1888 wing revision

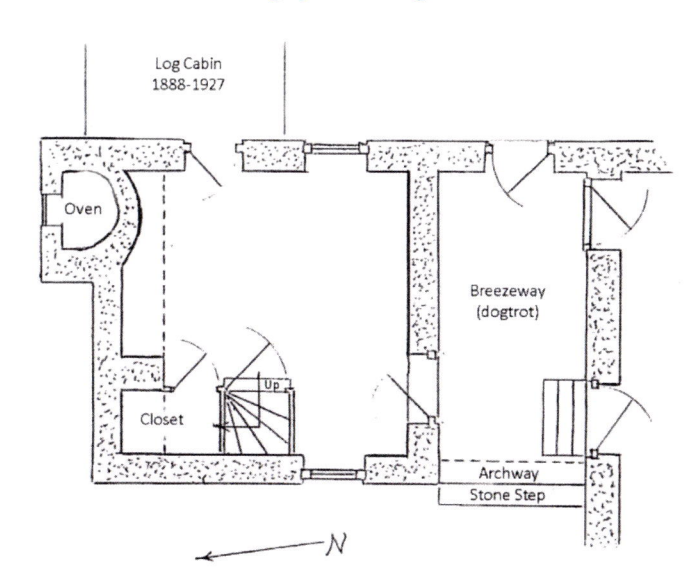

Drawing of wing floor plan 1888 until 1934

Log cabin addition from southeast after 1888 restoration

Log cabin addition from northwest after 1888 restoration

Finally, determined to resurrect that mysterious log cabin, the restorers built one projecting from the rear (northeast) corner of the kitchen.[7]

Why the restorers did this to the wing is shrouded in darkness, surely forever. It is conceivable that the "stone annex" which was to be torn down and replaced with a log cabin was the extension behind the wing appearing in the 1861 photograph; but visual examination shows that the annex was built of wood and brick. Most likely the intention was to demolish the main stone wing and build something like the log extension in the 1840 print which was displayed on the invitation to the centennial celebration. The Association knew that the existing wing was not an original part of the house, and this led them to guess that Martha Washington's "log cabben" must formerly have been on that site. Others had already come to that conclusion, such as Benson Lossing and Sherman Day. What caused the radical change in course is unknown.

One clue was the pent eave on the north. Its marks are clearly visible in the 1861 photograph. As they began their demolition, they would have found that the marks extended the full width of the house, showing that the eave had been removed to make room for the raised wing roof. While this would not preclude a one-story log cabin, further down the north wall of the main house, perhaps behind plaster, they doubtless found an imprint of an earlier wing roof. The stone work of the side walls may also have shown a junction between the lower walls of the early wing and the extensions erected during James Jones' ownership.

Other clues were inevitably revealed. On the floor level, as the workmen stripped out the decayed joists, they would have found the foundations of an earlier wall, the one-time separation between the original kitchen and the dogtrot. This wall was removed to enlarge the kitchen in the Jones' remodeling. As for the arched opening to the breezeway, a letter by Mrs. Conrad Jones about 1930 to the architectural historian, Horace Wells Sellers, sheds a rare glimmer of light. Mrs. Jones, the daughter of Theodore Bean, who was one of three on the restoration committee of 1887, recalled a visit to Valley Forge during the work. Her father pointed out a brick arch extending between the kitchen and the main house which was uncovered during demolition.[8] This obviously established the pattern for the arch which was incorporated into the restored wing.

Drawing of brick arch, ca. 1888

It can only be assumed, logically, that the evidence uncovered in this first restoration was so compelling that the restorers were obliged to deviate sharply from their original plan of action. The alterations in the wing were structurally quite radical. Aside from the physical clues which guided their work, the restoration team may have been enlightened from another source. It is possible that an elderly resident remembered the appearance of the house before the first renovation. Nathan Jones, whose father was probably the one to alter the wing originally and whom the Association dealt with on land, could have shed much light.

The Association felt that it had achieved its ultimate purpose: to restore the headquarters to what it was when Washington slept there. The story-and-a-half knee-walled wing with arch and breezeway was architecturally a far more convincing appendage than the massive, "country" primitive, two-story structure which it replaced. There was now visual balance, and the more refined detailing was in harmony with the town house formality of the main body. The wide arched opening joining a dependency to the main house, although not commonplace in Pennsylvania, occurred frequently enough. The architect G. Edwin Brumbaugh, an authority on historical buildings and promoter of the so-called Colonial Revival, describes an 18th century house in nearby Roxborough which had a wing with lowered roof and arched breezeway remarkably similar to that of the Potts house. This house had, unfortunately, been demolished some years earlier.[9]

The restoration work by the Centennial and Memorial Association was not above criticism in some particulars. When clear evidence was lacking, the restoration team was inclined to improvise in a cavalier manner. Having been frustrated in building a log cabin in place of the stone wing, it was determined to build one somewhere. That somewhere was on the site of the mid 19th century wood and brick annexes behind the kitchen. Whether this had historical warrant cannot be unequivocally denied, but it is highly dubious, as will be clear later in the chapter. The prototype sash for the oculus in the south gable had no doubt long since disappeared. With no model to guide them, the restorers designed their own, a wagon-wheel pattern with spokes radiating from a center point, and constructed it of 1887 period muntins and sash members. This sash, still in place, is attractive but not appropriate to the period of the house. It is also most likely that the 1887 restorers were responsible for the brick arched caps over the chimney tops. These hoods may have been for the practical purpose of keeping rain out, for there was no specific historical justification. They also were intrusive and a dubious aesthetic contribution.

The occasional derelictions stand out more vividly in contrast to the excellent work in general. Wherever sashes were replaced, the originals were copied so faithfully that the replacements are indistinguishable from originals. The same can be said for doors and shutters. On the other hand, the kitchen floor was replaced with late 19th century narrow-strip flooring. The old kitchen fireplace was also rehabilitated, doubtless after removal of a modern cook stove. But the masonry oven as reconstructed did not follow conventions of the house's era, having its opening on the exterior of the chimney, not the back wall of the fireplace. The inspiration for this deviation is unknown. The old lime mortar joints were unquestionably in urgent need of re-pointing when the restoration was made. It appears that a cement mortar was used which totally altered the appearance of the stonework. An extruded ribbon effect was imposed in the new mortar, a technique which was strictly Victorian.

On balance, however, the Association restorers' work was creditable. In the United States at least, restoration theory was still in its infancy in the 1880s. The ideal of total faithfulness to authenticity, to precise detail, had not evolved to the level of purity demanded by specialists of a later generation. But, as will be shortly revealed, a later generation was capable of even greater aberrations in its quest for authenticity.

For 17 years the Centennial and Memorial Association administered the headquarters, gradually adding to the property surrounding the original parcel. A strip was added between the house tract and the railroad as well as segments due south of the house which eventually encompassed the stone stable, the Nathan Jones house and the stone barn. The Nathan Jones land east of the house was finally acquired for

$1,200. The organization's financial position improved through infusions from a variety of sources. In 1890, Colonel Theodore Bean, as a member of the restoration committee, floated the idea of purchasing the entire encampment ground at a cost of about $100,000. The money would be raised through a bond with subscriptions open only to members of the Patriotic Order Sons of America, paying an interest of three per cent. The grandiose design attracted much interest but was tabled for the time being.

During the years of the Association the numbers of visitors swelled, thereby swelling the coffers of the organization as it charged the sightseers the admission fee of ten cents to visit the headquarters. This provided means to maintain the building. Various chapters of the Daughters of the American Revolution vied with each other for the privilege of furnishing rooms on the second floor and attic. Not all officers of the Association were happy over relinquishing control over what went into the shrine, voting a dissent on a number of applications. The majority approved the offers, perhaps considering it impolitic to offend the D.A.R.

The warden, or caretaker, was one Ellis Hampton who lived in the so-called janitor's lodge just southwest of the headquarters. He appears in a photograph from this period, standing before the house. His young son and a neighbor lad, later the architect G. Edwin Brumbaugh, served as guides to visitors, telling lurid tales of the underground passage to the river, sometimes earning nickel tips. It seems that the secret passage and the secret window seat compartment in Washington's office were by far the two most interesting objects to the public. While there actually is a window seat compartment, no one had ever seen Washington's tunnel to the river.

Warden standing by Headquarters, ca. 1900

On the 30th of May, 1893, the Pennsylvania State Legislature established the Valley Forge Park Commission, whose objectives were the same as the Centennial and Memorial Association: to purchase land of the old encampment and preserve it as a park forever. The legislature's act specifically excepted Washington's headquarters which was owned by the Association. On the 19th of June, the stockholders of the Association graciously invited the new Park Commission to use the headquarters house for meeting purposes whenever necessary, a courtesy that was not reciprocated a few years later. By the middle of the next year it became clear to the Association that the Park Commission had designs on the headquarters, to take over the property and add it to the park domain. In support of this, state advocates for the proposed acquisition argued that it was not proper for admission to be charged to visit the headquarters, since the public was admitted free to other Washington shrines around the country. The Association was determined to resist this and to maintain control of the headquarters.

The determination was all for naught. In 1905, without even notifying the Association, the state legislature revised its Act of 1893, now giving the Commission power to condemn the headquarters property and secure it for the Park. The Association was embittered by what it saw as the State's high-handedness and initially sought to contest the action by all legal means. When the futility of this became clear, the Association asked at least $25,000 in damages, but a jury of review finally awarded it $18,000. Again seeing the writing on the wall, the Association asked that a plaque be installed in the headquarters giving tribute to the work of the Centennial and Memorial Association and that $200 compensation be paid for furnishing, books, painting, and souvenirs remaining in the headquarters. After first refusing the plaque, the Commission finally assented, but the request for $200 was quibbled over at great length.

The condemnation went through and the $18,000 was awarded to the Association. The State of

Pennsylvania was now the custodian of the headquarters. The old Association laid plans for its own dissolution. It asked permission to meet in its old room in the headquarters, but the State Commission turned it down. So it met in the Washington Inn nearby, David Potts' house. The Association wanted to distribute the balance of $16,000 to its members upon dissolution, but the State demanded that the money be turned over to the Valley Forge Park Commission as proper successor to the Association. Once again the Association lost, the courts contending the corporation (Association) was non-profit, and that as its fund was for a charitable and patriotic purpose, it could not be subverted from the stated purpose. The state did guarantee that the money would be used strictly for maintenance of the headquarters house and environs. The Centennial and Memorial Association dissolved, leaving behind a commemorative tablet on the headquarters wall and a privately published history of its work.[10] The Valley Forge Park Commission could pride itself on inheriting a restored house and $16,000. "This large sum was in this manner secured for the benefit of the State by alertness and activity on the part of the Commission."[11]

Although the new Park Commission early announced its intention to restore the interior of the headquarters to its condition during Washington's residence, its initial efforts were toward environmental improvement. By 1910, the ruins of the old mill were removed, eliminating an eyesore. Whether these were the ruins of the 1760 Potts grist mill or, more likely, of an 1844 grist mill built slightly to the south was not specified. At the same time, the Victorian-style janitor's lodge built by the Centennial and Memorial Association was slated for destruction.[12]

Little alteration was made in the headquarters until after 1920. In 1914, it was painted inside and out, and a program was undertaken to furnish the house with articles of the revolutionary times. There had been no central heating before 1919, when a hot water system was installed both for the guests and "to prevent injury to the walls and plaster," no doubt from dampness. To avoid any fire hazard to the old house, a furnace and boiler were placed in the Commission's offices (Nathan Jones' house) with water piped underground to radiators in the open fireplaces of the headquarters.[13]

By the mid 1920s, as the commemoration of the 150th year of the encampment was drawing near, the Park Commission became active in bringing greater authenticity to the historical scene. It engaged the highly respected historical architect, Horace Wells Sellers, chairman of the Committee on Historic Monuments of the Philadelphia Chapter of the American Institute of Architects, to direct the program. In 1926 and 1927, major changes were carried out.

As for the surroundings, the Potts house stable was shorn of 19th century gewgaws and turned into a museum.

Just to its south, the Nathan Jones house was "colonialized," its mansard replaced by a gable roof. This was by no means a "restoration" but simply to make the building look more in harmony with its recreated 18th century neighborhood. Odds and ends of architectural trash were torn down. Archaeologists made renewed efforts to locate traces of ancient iron forges and vanished mills.

The Sellers committee turned to the headquarters as well. The decorative cement pointing of the first restoration was rubbed out, replaced with a rough-tooled pointing believed to be more appropriate to the colonial period. The plastered jambs and soffit of the breezeway arch were chipped clean. The log cabin annex of 1887 was demolished after the restorers claimed that it had been fabricated of discarded telegraph poles, the chinks filled with modern lath and plaster. In the kitchen, "the floor of narrow pine boards was taken up and a brick floor substituted, and the kitchen once more assumed the appearance of a kitchen instead of part of a museum."[14] A picket fence was built, rose trellises placed against the south wall (as they had been in the early photographs), and a general prettification of the milieu was carried out. For the time being the headquarters house remained substantially unchanged.

This was soon to change. By 1927, Sellers and his committee had concluded that the house in its current form was not the domicile Washington knew. They were now aware of the early photographs and engravings described in the previous chapter. For some reason, Sellers put great reliance on remembrances of Jerome Sheas, the elderly Park superintendent who knew the headquarters before the 1887 restoration. Sheas, naturally, could only recall the kitchen wing as it appeared in the mid 19th century photographs and engravings.

Sellers said in his memorandum that:

Mr. Sheas stated that from his recollection of the original kitchen wing, it had the appearance of a building existing before the main house was built, being similar to pre-revolutionary houses of the neighborhood. That he knows of no authority for the building that has replaced it and that the house must have had a kitchen before the traditional log cabin addition was built. At all events, during his long experience at Valley Forge, he recalls nothing that seems to justify the construction of the kitchen wing as it now appears.[15]

Why Sellers would have given so much importance to the testimony of a man whose memory could not have extended back further than the 1870s or 1880s is incomprehensible. In contrast to Day and Lossing, who believed the wing was a more modern structure, Sheas and Sellers now thought it may have predated the main house. This opinion, in fact, was a prevalent one at this time, based to some extent on readings or misreadings of early documentation on the property. When John Potts acquired the lands in 1758, there were references to a "pioneer" house on the mill tract. Theories that the pioneer house may have been the two story wing to which Potts then added the main body of the house had, apparently, become widely believed at the time Sellers was doing his work. By this logic, Sellers could easily conclude that the pre-1887 two-story wing had been present when Washington occupied the house. The work of the Centennial and Memorial Association was thus rendered incomprehensible and was summarily dismissed.[16]

    The inquiry into the kitchen wing had less happy results. Sellers made a sincere effort to find records of the Centennial and Memorial Association to learn why it did so in the first restoration. The only response was the letter from Theodore Bean's daughter. Her report on the brick arch did not convince Sellers, who could detect no evidence of it in the 1861 photograph. In the absence of other persuasive evidence to the contrary, Sellers concluded that the wing of the early photographs and the old engravings was the true and original one and that the work of the Centennial and Memorial Association should be undone.

    Some features of his reasoning are worthy of note. He did not think it likely that, if the kitchen had originally been a semi-detached appendage, the arch would have been used on only one end of the breezeway. That is, a matching arch would logically have appeared on the east wall also, making the dogtrot a true dogtrot. Moreover, the dogtrot reduced the kitchen to a tiny room, quite overwhelmed by a disproportionately large fireplace. If, as Sellers believed, there had never been a dogtrot and the kitchen extended the full length of the wing, the room would have been more practical, both for cooking and for a dining table, "a not uncommon practice where the farm hands as well as the household had to be so accommodated."[17]

The flaws in Sellers' reasoning may be more obvious retrospectively, but they are vivid indeed. The brick arch is not visible in the 1861 photograph, but the whitewashing or plastering of the wall would have disguised it. He nevertheless chose to discount it. However logical an arched opening at both ends of the breezeway may be, another such illogical example was presented at the nearby Peter Wentz house in which the summer kitchen is attached by a dogtrot with a large arched opening on one end and a solid wall with a window on the other. Sellers may not have been familiar with this example, but that would be most surprising for an historical architect.

John and Cherry Dodds, in their "Historic Structure Report," detail other curious aberrations. Why did Sellers ignore the obvious removal of the north pent eave to make room for the (later) raised wing? His decision to place a brick floor in the kitchen suggests that he did not investigate the early joist pockets in the kitchen walls. Had he done so, he would have uncovered evidence of the early wing configuration which would have challenged the conclusions he reached. His idea that a larger kitchen would have been necessary for dining by the family alongside its farm hands was especially flawed. The Potts house was not a farm house. The kitchen would only have been used by cooks and servants. Complaining about cramped quarters was presumably not a habit of slaves and servants in that period. The well-to-do Potts family would not have dined cheek by jowl with its servants, but used only the dining room in the main house. Finally, as already noted, Sellers placed much stock in the testimony by Jerome Sheas whose memory did not extend back nearly far enough to be of significance in the early history of the house.

  By 1931, it is clear that Sellers had concluded that all evidence documentary, logical, and hearsay, suggested another restoration was in order, that is, a resurrection of something as close as possible to the pre-1887 wing. The search for old records of the previous work had led to nothing, so in the absence of information or evidence to the contrary, he and his committee decided to persuade the Park Commission to approve the project, which it did. In 1931, a draftsman by the name of L. H. Sellers (relation to Horace Wells Sellers is not known) prepared a fine set of complete architectural drawings of the house as it then existed. Sheet 21 was a preliminary floor plan of the proposed reconstruction. The drawing was obviously based on careful studies of the 1861 photograph, which is the only known photograph from the period that clearly shows the wing.

The work was not commenced immediately, but in 1934 it went forward. This, in the depth of the Depression, and no small inducement to the project, was the chance to put skilled stone masons, carpenters, and plasterers back to work. The roof on the story-and-a-half wing was not demolished but raised to the full two-story level. This time the pent eave on the north gable of the main building was not wholly removed but notched to accommodate the wing roof.

The stone wall dividing the kitchen from the breezeway was knocked out, and the arched opening on the front wall was filled in again, eliminating the dogtrot. The kitchen windows were raised considerably to harmonize with their apparent level in the old photograph. To maintain proportions, the floor of the kitchen was elevated about a foot, the brick paving of 1926 being re-laid on a dirt and sand fill. This brought the floor even with, or slightly above, the grade outside, not a step below as it had been formerly.

On the new second floor a small bedroom (without fireplace) and an anteroom were connected to the main house by opening a door to the stairway landing, but an enclosed service stair also descended directly to the kitchen.

So, the wing went through its second major revision within 50 years, further eliminating any traces

*View showing wing with dogtrot eliminated
and full two stories – 1952*

of what may have been the original wing. Perhaps the only residue remaining of the original wing was the lower parts of the walls. However, the brick arch soffit which guided the first restorers was demolished and disappeared forever.

Observers of the 1861 wing, such as Day and Lossing, noted that it appeared crude and primitive compared to the main building. The restorers of the 1930s consciously made the detailing more refined, more in harmony, they believed, with the main house. But the restoration also looked new. Whatever rust of authenticity the pre-1887 wing may have had, was not, and could not be, reproduced.

Very little, beyond routine maintenance, was done to the headquarters for the next 40 years. Some flooring was replaced with planks recycled from nearby historical demolitions.

However, in furnishing and landscaping, every effort went to make the headquarters the well-appointed, elegantly tasteful home of a modest late 18th century patrician. The white picket fence surrounded a neatly manicured lawn, and profuse plantings such as dogwoods flourished all about the environs. Trellises on the south wall also supported flowering vines. In all, the headquarters setting sought to recapture what a prosperous Isaac Potts of 1784 would supposedly have seen within and outside his home.

The ongoing quest for historical authenticity brought the interior colors of the house into question as midcentury approached. Until that time, decorating schemes reflected what in the early century was considered typical "colonial" colors, white painted woodwork and neutral painted walls. Researchers then became increasingly aware of the rich, even gaudy, colors which were common in late 18th century interiors. G. Edwin Brumbaugh, who in 1949 directed a restoration of the David Potts' house was asked by the Park Commission also to investigate the headquarters' colors.

His wife Frances, an interior decorator with wide experience in historical restoration, did some discreet scrapings. She unearthed the earliest paint layers, which she and her husband analyzed. They concluded that the early paneling had been far more colorful and variegated than previously thought.

Dining room picture from postcard ca. 1950 showing Brumbaugh colors

In a letter to the chairman of the Valley Forge Park Commission, Brumbaugh revealed the preliminary results of their inquiry. The paneling and woodwork in the parlor, entrance and stair hall, and the back (east) bedroom appeared originally to have been a dark mustard yellow. The dining room paneling was an earthen red, and the two front bedrooms were a deep, dark blue.

Approximate color swatches selected by Brumbaughs

As the kitchen wing was not original, the Brumbaughs had no primary evidence but assumed, based on precedent and experience, that the trim was a dark red. The walls throughout the house as well as the plastered facings on the fireplaces in the bedrooms and dining room were most likely pure white or slightly cream whitewash.[18]

In 1952, the redecorating was authorized, and the color pattern described above was reproduced under the authority of Mrs. Brumbaugh. Painting began in January, 1953, but had to be instantly halted when ceiling plaster gave way during paint removal. After re-plastering of ceilings throughout the structure, the work was completed. The rich color scheme determined by the Brumbaughs to be historical remained unchanged for over 20 more years, and the house otherwise underwent little beyond routine maintenance.

Headquarters with cannon as of 1954

In 1976, a serious reconsideration of the Brumbaugh work was undertaken as will be discussed later.

Further questions over authenticity continued to accumulate, however, and the approach of the Revolutionary Bicentennial brought them to the fore. Custody of the Park had been transferred to the Pennsylvania Historical and Museum Commission.

The Commission launched an ambitious program of research and restoration of the major historic structures throughout the Park, an undertaking to be done in time for the Bicentennial of the encampment, 1977-78. Washington's headquarters, of course, was to be included. An architectural/restoration firm, National Heritage Corporation of West Chester, Pennsylvania, was awarded the contract to handle the entire project.

Historical archaeology led off the investigation. In the summer of 1973, a team of student archaeologists furnished by National Heritage and led by an archaeologist of the Commission did diggings around the headquarters, registering signs of soil displacement, buried foundations, and artifacts.

One specific objective was to locate, if possible, structural remnants of the legendary log cabin dining room mentioned by Martha Washington. These, it was hoped, could be guides to reconstruction of some sort of replica. Nothing was discovered which could be confirmed as residue of that long-vanished log structure, so this part of the project was wisely abandoned.

Diggings to the east and south of the house revealed an old fill of perhaps 14 inches depth. Even though the probes were no closer than 15 feet to the east wall of the headquarters, it led the restorers to believe that the historical grade around the house had been dramatically lower than it was in 1973. This was the justification for eventually scraping off a foot to 18 inches of top soil around most of the structure. The dubiousness of this action will be discussed presently.

A most significant result of the archaeological inquiry was yet another revision of the then existing kitchen wing. Even at this late date, questions about the possibility of a log structure predating the stone wing continued to hover about.

Another unexplored theory was that of Sellers and others, which hypothesized that the two-story wing of 1861 was actually an earlier structure to which the main body of the house was later added. The team set to work excavating the brick-paved first floor of the kitchen.

The bricks laid down in the 1934 restoration were removed, followed by nearly a foot of yellow clay fill. This revealed a concrete slab with marks of the bricks corresponding exactly to their arrangement in the floor of 1934. The lower floor on the concrete slab would have been the work of the Sellers restoration of the 1920s. This slab was broken up, exposing rocky fill interspersed with concrete beams.

The beams apparently supported the wood plank floor laid in the 1897 restoration, the concrete members doubtless replacing the original wood joists which had rotted. When sterile subsoil was reached, a foot-and-a-half of material had been removed from the surface of the 1973 kitchen floor.[19]

The discoveries in this dig provided important guidelines to restoration proceedings. No artifacts were uncovered dating prior to the last quarter of the 18th century, even though the archaeologists were unable to vouchsafe that no earlier structure had stood on the site of the wing. More significant were pockets for wooden joists found in the sidewalls.

Assuming that the sidewalls, at that low level, were original, the pockets showed that the original floor had been wood planks. More important, the pockets did not extend the full length of the wing but terminated over eight feet north of the north wall of the main house.

This, as well as the mortared stone foundations of a wall beneath the south-most joist, indicated that the enclosed portion of the original kitchen was separated, or at least partially separated, from the main house. Between the mortared foundations of an original south wall of the kitchen and the main house had been an outdoor space, or at least a breezeway.

In the following drawing it will show what brought about this separation of the kitchen and the breezeway.

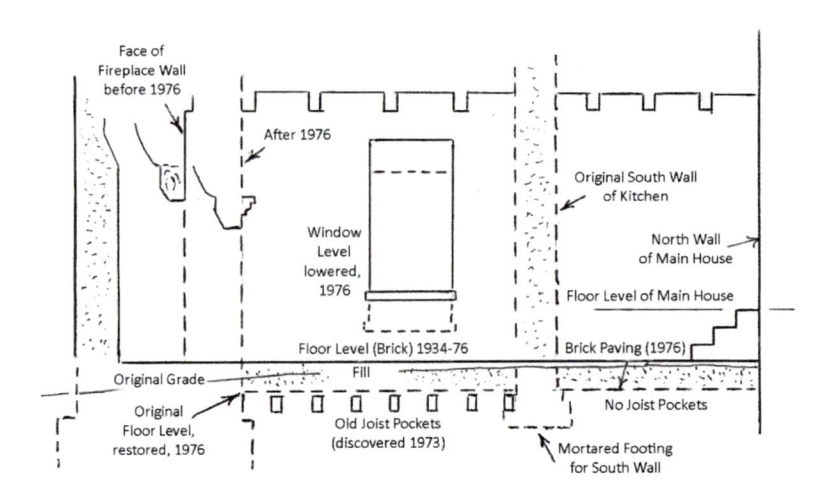

Drawing of original floor level of kitchen wing – during 1976 restoration

The archaeologist, Vance Packard, speculated that the wing of *ca.* 1887 to 1934, with the semi-detached kitchen, breezeway, and broad arch on the front, may have been the original configuration. He suggested that the arched doorway on the west wall of the old stable could have been a match to the original arch on the house wing. He cited a parallel arch with breezeway on the Peter Wentz house, 1758, to show that such arrangements were not unheard-of in the late 18th century. Packard implied that the Centennial and Memorial Association would hardly have undergone the great difficulty of fitting an arch into a pre-existent wall unless it had compelling evidence that such was original.[20]

Packard's conclusions on these matters were to be incorporated by the architects of the Bicentennial restoration.

There was also an archaeological confirmation of the previously described architectural analysis that placed the construction of the house after 1770. As Packard stated in his field notes: ". . . the apparent absence of any material dating earlier than the last quarter of the 18th century leads one to suspect that the building predates the Revolution by only a few years."

The stage was set for the third major restoration of Washington's headquarters in its history and the fourth renovation of its wing. In preparation for the bicentennial restoration, the State legislature appropriated $100,000. In 1976, the State of Pennsylvania bequeathed Valley Forge Park to the United States government, Department of the Interior. The custody of the Park has since been under the National Park Service. The Department of the Interior approved an additional $91,000 for the restoration.[21]

Beyond the archaeological evidence, what led the architects of National Heritage to revise the wing into its present form has been published in only sketchy form. As revealed above, the ancient joist pockets indicated that the original kitchen did not run the full length of the wing but was at least semi-detached. The 1798 Glass Tax, which recorded the kitchen as one-story in height, was known.[22]

The 1861 photograph showing traces of the missing north pent eave demonstrated that the two-story wing of 1861 was not original.

Beyond the primary evidence, it is conjectural to what extent the 1887-1933 wing guided the restorers of the mid 1970s who had access to all drawings and photographs of the earlier wing.

The wing as rebuilt bears strong resemblance to the pre-1933 incarnation. The roof was again lowered to almost exactly its level of 1887-1933. Some imprint of the earlier roof was doubtless still detectable on the north wall of the main house. As no other tracings were found, the 1976 restorers concluded that the 1887 roof was overlaid onto the original imprint.[23]

The floor of the kitchen and the dogtrot were lowered about a foot, joists placed in the original joist pockets, and a plank floor installed. Kitchen windows were accordingly lowered about ten inches to approximately their position before Seller's work.

The archaeological diggings revealed that the original fireplace footings were much larger than the existent fireplace demonstrated.

The newly-restored hearth was over two feet deeper than the former one, consuming even more floor space in the already tiny kitchen. Having no primary evidence to guide them, the restorers reconstructed the fireplace, overmantel, and beehive oven in a style consistent with the area and era.

Kitchen wing from north with beehive oven

View from northwest, 1976 restoration

The impossibility of authenticating any of the work of 1887, meant that the bicentennial restorers felt obliged to improvise on the basis of learned speculation with several details. For example, the arch on the west stable door was copied for the dogtrot opening under the assumption that the stable was contemporaneous with the house and that the builders would have made a match. The soffit of the 1887-1933 arch was of brick, which may well have been original. The chimney of the 1887-1933 kitchen was stone, but the 1976 restorers made it of brick, assuming that it would have been of the same material as the chimneys on the main house. Doubts could be cast on this.

Headquarters' stable showing arched opening

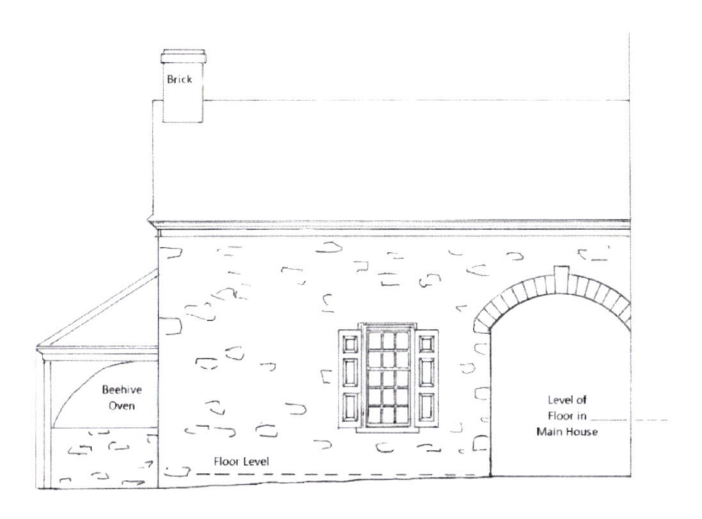

Drawing of elevation of 1976 restored wing

  The most curious decision was to make the ceiling level nearly equal to the wing's walls, making the ceiling height approximately ten feet, disproportionate for such a small room. The Centennial Association had recreated a one-and-a-half story knee-walled form with a window garret above a low-ceilinged kitchen. Architectural logic would favor the latter course, but again, the bicentennial restorers were most likely trying to avoid an uncritical copy of the earlier model. It could be argued that they fell into the trap of overcorrecting. Details aside, the 1976 restored wing, like the 1887-1933 version, was more in harmony with the main structure, more visually pleasing than the cumbersome, rather crude two-story enclosed form which existed just before 1887 and after its reproduction by Sellers in

1933. Far more important, of course, is that it is now deemed to be the form Washington knew in 1777-1778.

Kitchen as it is today

    Extensive detail work was done on the main house, most of a cosmetic nature. The rake molding on the north gable was revised to match the more elaborate rake on the south gable. First observable in the 1861 photograph, the north gable rake was merely a simple 1 x 5 inch trim board, whereas the south had a double ogee like the cornice molding, leading to a considerable roof overhang. Presumably the original north gable rake had deteriorated early in the building's history and had not been faithfully copied in the repair. The bicentennial team was the first to correct this imbalance. The stone work was totally re-pointed with a very white mortar extruded, or cupped, a bit beyond the face of the stone. The result is a rather aggressive joint pattern, but there were historical precedents.

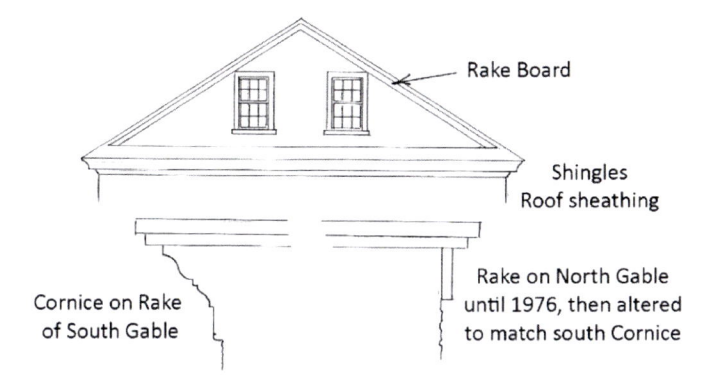

Drawing of details of rake boards of north and south gable before 1976

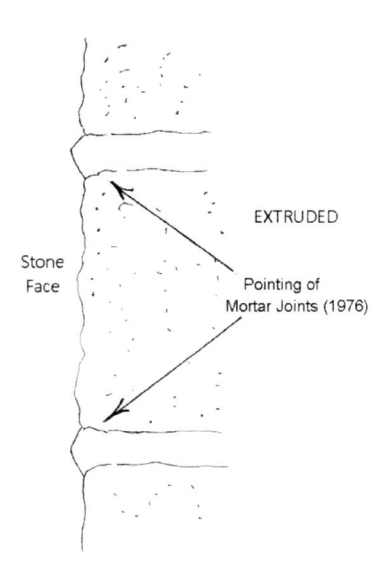

Drawing of pointing of mortar joints in 1976

Two revisions which had undoubted authority were the passageways to the basement. The original inside stairway, under the main staircase and opening onto the entrance hall beneath the landing, had been replaced sometime by a stair opening into the kitchen. This was probably done by James Jones who originally altered the wing. Finding the marks of the original stairway, the 1976 restorers replaced it and closed up the doorway into the kitchen (now breezeway). In the east wall of the basement, there was evidence of an outside passage through a trap door, an arrangement which had also been eliminated sometime in the murky past. The restorers reopened the door in the foundation wall and rebuilt the bulkhead with a trap door. For the first time in its history, the dirt floor of the basement was covered with a concrete slab, primarily as an effort to keep the house drier.

Rear view of house showing trap door

Bulkhead and Trapdoor

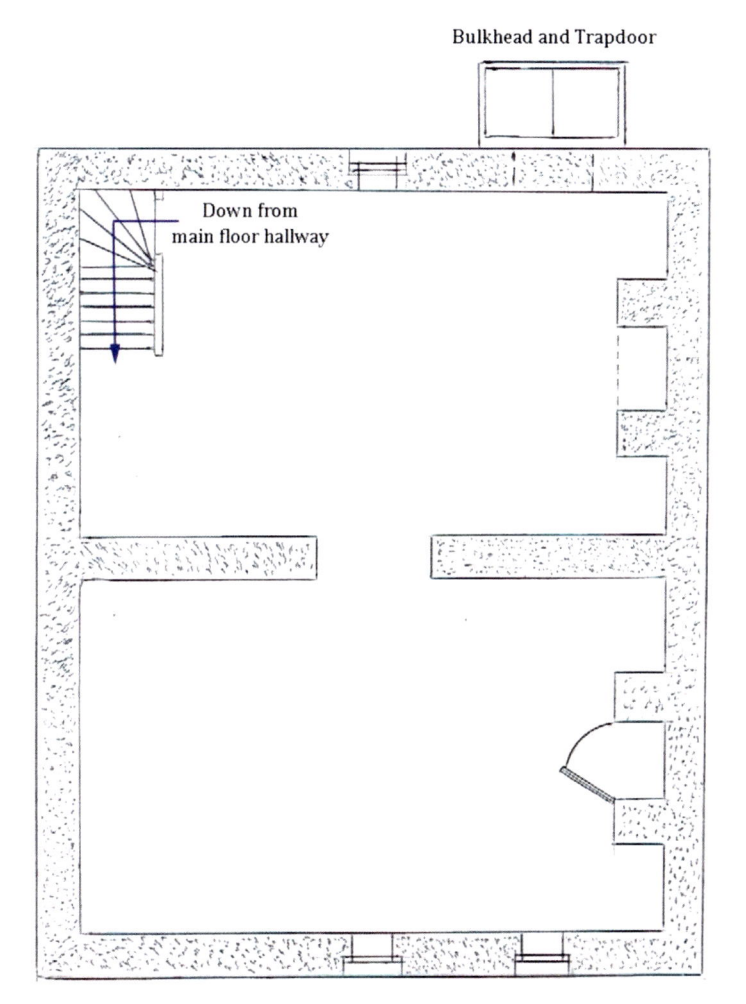

Down from main floor hallway

FRONT OF HOUSE

Drawing of basement plan

Other interior work was directed toward repairing the ravages of hordes of visitors. Door hinges and locks were largely replaced by modern reproductions. Much badly worn flooring, especially in the hallways, was replaced and then stained to resemble old planks.

Repainting was also in order, but colors used by the late Frances Brumbaugh in 1953 had been custom-mixed, and to match them from her husband's surviving samples was not practical. The National Heritage Corporation thus commissioned a paint expert to repeat the earlier research. His scrapings and microscopic laboratory analysis revealed original colors considerably different from the Brumbaugh findings. The most vivid contrasts were in the upstairs and downstairs east rooms. The exterior trim was also investigated, and it was discovered that the original windows and doors were of a creamy hue rather than dead white. The new colors were utilized throughout the 1976 repainting. All the colors used were keyed to a standardized color notation system which will facilitate matching in future repainting. G. Edwin Brumbaugh was not impressed by the results, insisting that the work of his late wife and himself had already established the colors that were "historically correct."[24]

The most dubious alteration during the restoration was the re-grading of the soil around the house. Ostensibly because the archaeological team found evidence of fill some distance behind the structure, the conclusion was drawn that the modern grade around the house was considerably higher than it was in the early days. On this supposition, anywhere from one foot to 18 inches of soil were scraped away. The cellar windows, both front and back, which had previously been partially submerged and protected by stone wells, were now totally above grade. Visually, the house acquired a conspicuously taller, nearly gaunt, aspect. Was this radical revision justified?

South end showing foundation stones exposed in re-grading in 1976

  On the weight of evidence, the answer would have to be no. Before re-grading, the ground around the house had a gentle slope northwest toward the river, from the highest point on the southeast corner of the house to the lowest point, the northwest corner of the kitchen wing. At the latter location, the ground and original kitchen floor would have been at about the same level, meaning that much of the kitchen floor was below grade. In the 1887-1934 version of the house, the breezeway floor at the arched opening was one step down from ground level. On the east, at the opposite end of the breezeway, there was a three-step difference. The Dodds, in their "Historic Structure Report," suspected that the real reason behind lowering the grade in 1976, was reluctance to have a kitchen floor below grade. However flawed that may be from the structural viewpoint, it was a frequent practice in the 18th century.[25] In the previous restoration, Sellers' aversion to such a practice led him to raise the kitchen floor at least a foot.

Evidence that the landscape change was unwarranted is compelling. Careful scrutiny of the 1861 photograph shows the grade at the time to have been identical to what it was just before 1976. This is best seen in the number of steps to the front stoop. Admittedly, 1861 was not 1773, but when would the radical change have taken place?

It likely never did, as revealed by the stonework itself. Lowering the grade exposed a coarse stone pattern altogether unlike the more refined work immediately above it. Small stones laid in a hodge-podge, some even projecting a few inches beyond the plane of the wall, prove that the mason never intended this portion of the wall to be anything but subterranean foundation. The line of demarcation is quite clear, and it corresponds with the pre-1976 soil level, so the 1976 re-grading stripped away the historical ground cover, doing remarkable violence to the aesthetic proportions of the house. In the course of time, another grader will most likely be commissioned to restore the historical contour. But artifacts that may have been scraped away with the original soil can never be reclaimed. It is conceivable that some item among the ancient detritus now lost could have helped date the house.[26]

Northwest corner of main house, showing foundation stones exposed by 1976 re-grading

  With re-grading, reconstruction of the wing, "ridge pointing" of all the mortar joints with a very white mortar, replacement of hardware, and the fresh paint, the headquarters took on a deceptive "newness" which harmonized with the Park Service's effort to give the illusion that it is 1777-1778 again. The newness is further enhanced by the barren setting of the house, the result of stripping away picket fences, flowering plants, and shrubbery that gave the pre-1976 scene a residential luxuriance, a "Better Homes and Gardens" aspect. Vegetation consisted only of unbroken, neatly-mown lawn, and a few ancient trees.

The tidy starkness does not, of course, reproduce what would have been the 18th-century appearance. The grist- and saw mills, which then so dominated the area, cannot be reconstructed, for there is no documentation of their appearances. The old State Park and the present National Historical Park have wisely refrained from attempting strictly imaginary replicas. The fencing of the encampment period and the impact of omnipresent grazing livestock are also impossible to represent accurately, both through insufficient information and the relentless need to accommodate hordes of visitors. Sawbuck or snake fences are routinely positioned about to give an impression of old-fashioned rusticity.

As for the headquarters house, the Park Service has put much energy into authenticating its furnishings and providing maximum accessibility to the public. Courteous and well-informed interpreters, sometimes in period costume, now present brief verbal introductions to visitors, giving basic information about the headquarters during the encampment and answering questions. In the old State Park days, room entrances were covered by locked grilled gates, but today low barriers (with electronic alarms) open up the rooms to easier viewing.

Furnishing is now designed to capture the scene during the actual encampment. Historic camp furniture is stuffed into the rooms, suggesting what must have been the congestion of that time. Antique items are freely used, but, to keep the rooms from turning into display chambers for historic furniture, reproductions are commonplace as well. In short, the stage-setting is conceived of as more important than the individual pieces.[27]

 A minor practical innovation within the last ten years was placement of tinted plexiglass sheets over the inside of all windows. These are, in effect, storm windows to reduce heat wastage through the drafty old sashes. The tinting is to reduce the ultraviolet light so injurious to antique wood and fabrics. While these emplacements were designed to be as innocuous as possible, they have some unfortunate effects. The tinting casts a permanent, unnatural gloom over the interior, somewhat subverting the goal of giving a lifelike "feel" to the scene. Also, while less conspicuous than exterior storms, the plastic sheets are conspicuous enough, obscuring the attractive interior detailing of the sash. As so often, when economy and preservation are key concerns, the necessary compromises invariably shortchange aesthetic considerations.

 Other than routine maintenance and repairs, no significant alterations have been done to the house since the bicentennial restoration. This is fortunate. While there remain questions of authenticity, particularly with regard to the wing, the house has already suffered far too many "revisions." Every restoration has destroyed more of whatever artifactual residues once existed. The present wing is an approximation of the form recreated by the Centennial and Memorial Association. No doubt the earlier incarnation was, in detail, closer to the original, simply because the 1887 restorers had much more evidence to guide them. The unfortunate Sellers restoration of 1934 destroyed most of that. Except for re-grading of the soil around the house, it is probably best to leave well enough alone. Barring the miraculous and improbable discovery of now unknown historical documentation, any additional radical surgery would have to be based largely on guesswork. There has been too much of that already.

The artisans of 220 years ago, who crafted the Potts house, could never have imagined the destiny of their creation. They could not even have envisioned what it was soon to witness during the War for Independence, let alone the changes in human life over the subsequent two centuries. The structure survived because of its good fortune, inherent sturdiness, the loving efforts of generations dedicated to preservation, and in spite of all-too-human heedlessness and misjudgment. Admittedly, its preservation was not by virtue of its qualities, but through an accident of history. Yet, to those who cherish its intrinsic appeal, it stands, with unperturbed dignity, as a silent monument to a long-vanished world of order, taste, and honest craftsmanship.

EPILOGUE

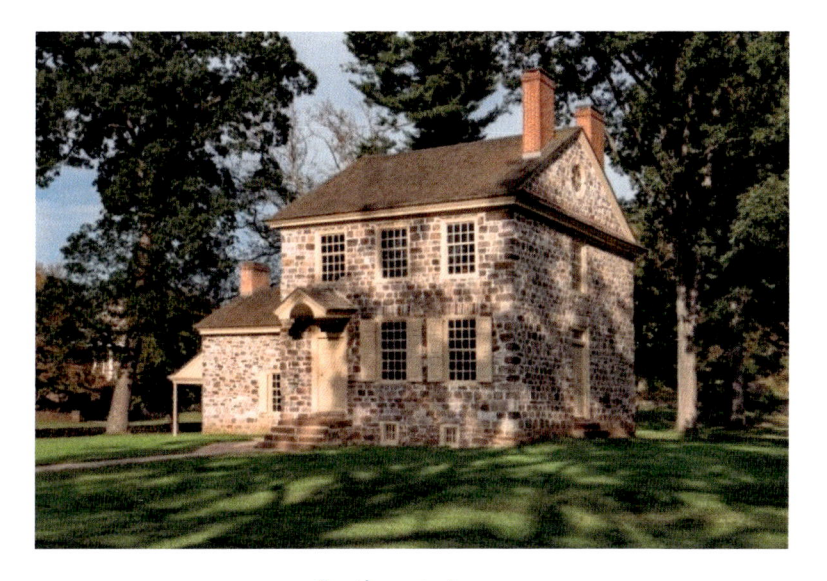

Southwest view

    By the 1880s, a patriotic spirit was stirring the land; mementos of the American Revolution and expressed respect for the heroes of the War for Independence were becoming increasingly numerous. The patriotic organization, The Centennial and Memorial Association, wanted to glorify people and places connected with the days of George Washington. One of its quests was to purchase the Valley Forge Headquarters and have it open to the public on the memorial days. This, it accomplished, and climaxed its good services by carrying out a major restoration of the

Potts house. Their reconstruction of what was undoubtedly the original kitchen wing unquestionably restored much of the charm and balance to the structure. For a generation, a Pennsylvania State Historical Park guarded the house and its environs. One more botched restoration of the house in the 1930s was mercifully treated by a professional restoration firm in time for the commemoration of the Bicentennial in 1976.

So, Isaac Potts' old house has been providentially spared for our time. It is a relic of a birth moment in our nation's history. It symbolizes an increasingly sophisticated advancement in techniques of professional historic preservation. It is a beautiful conformation, rich with Georgian details, illustrating creative skills of a now long vanished generation.

CHRONOLOGICAL HIGHLIGHTS OF HEADQUARTERS EVENTS

1743 to 1976

1743
    The iron works (Mount Joy Forge) operation begun just east of Valley Creek.

1757
    John Potts (1710-1768) becomes owner of the iron works (including a tract of 175 acres).

1760 or later, possibly as late as 1770
    A house is built that is later used by Washington as the headquarters during the encampment.

1768
    John Potts dies. Several changes of ownership regarding his children.

1771
    William Dewees manages the forge, David Potts is in Philadelphia doing marketing.

1773
    Isaac Potts becomes owner of the grist mill.

1777-1778
    Winter encampment at Valley Forge.

June 19th, 1778
    Evacuation of Washington's army from Valley Forge.

1806-1826
    HQ house owned by Joseph Paul.

About 1826-1849
: HQ house owned by James Jones and family. Jones encloses the original kitchen and adds a full second story to it.

About 1850-1877
: HQ house owned by Hannah Jones Ogden (James Jones' daughter).

1878
: Founding of Centennial and Memorial Association to prepare for centennial and acquire headquarters for preservation.

1886
: Centennial and Memorial Association receives deed for headquarters house.

1887
: Association restores headquarters, reducing kitchen wing from two to 1 ½ stories and inserting dogtrot and arch between kitchen and main house.

1893
: Establishment of Valley Forge Park Commission (beginning of Valley Forge State Park).

1905
: Condemnation and acquisition of headquarters by Park Commission. Property added to State Park.

Late 1920s
: Preparations for Sesquicentennial. Minor restorations on headquarters and surroundings directed by Horace Welles Sellers (architect).

1934 to 1936

    Second restoration of headquarters under direction of Sellers, et. al. Wing raised to resemble pre-1887 form, full two-story and closed-kitchen running full length of wing.

1973

    Beginning of preparation for Bicentennial; archaeological explorations.

1976

    Valley Forge State Park acquired by U.S. Government, Department of Interior, making it Valley Forge National Historical Park.

    Third restoration of headquarters, again reducing height of wing to one story and reintroducing arch and dogtrot. House again resembles 1887 restoration.

NOTES

CHAPTER ONE: 18TH CENTURY MATRIX

1. Woodman. *The History of the Valley Forge*. pp. 27-28.

2. Bining. *Pennsylvania Iron Manufacturers in the18th Century.*

3. James. *Memorial of Thomas Potts, Junior*. p. 104.

4. Stone. *The Mount Joy Forge on Valley Creek*. p. 96.

5. James. *Memorial.* p. 150.

6. Philadelphia County Will No.189. Norristown: Montgomery County Court House.

7. James. *Memorial.* p.108.

8. Ibid., p. 219.

9. Stone. *Mount Joy Forge.* p. 97.

10. James. *Memorial.* p. 220.

11. National Heritage Corporation. "Historical Research Valley Forge State Park." 1974. p. 51. Valley Forge National Historical Park Library. Philadelphia County Tax Assessment Ledgers, 1773, p. 226, and 1774, p. 225.

12. Treese. *Valley Forge – Making and Remaking a National Symbol.* p. 20.

13. James. *Memorial.* p. 219.

14. Dodd. *Historic Structure Report, Washington's Headquarters.* p. 19.

15. National Heritage Corporation. p. 49.

16. "The Pennsylvania Gazette." Philadelphia, February 7, 1776. In Pennsylvania Historical Society.

17. Menz. *Historic Furnishings Report: Washington's Headquarters.* p. 14.

CHAPTER TWO: WAR COMES TO THE VALLEY

1. Stone. *Mount Joy Forge.* pp. 115-116.

2. Ibid., p. 118.

3. Washington. *The Writings of George Washington from the Original Manuscript Sources, 1745-1799*, ed. John Fitzpatrick. Washington: U. S. Government Printing Office, 1933. p. X 149.

4. Ibid., 1934. p. XI 268.

5. James. *Memorial.* p. 219.

6. "Warren-Adams Papers," Massachusetts Historical Society, Boston.

7. Drinker. "Elizabeth Drinker Journal," April 16, 1778, Historical Society of Pennsylvania, Philadelphia.

8. Boudinot. *Journal or Historical Recollections of American Events During the Revolutionary War.* pp. 77-78.

9. Menz. *Historic Furnishings.* pp. 3-4.

10. Chastellux. *Travels in North America.* p. 514.

CHAPTER THREE: THE POTTS HOUSE, A STUDY

1. Sellers, L.H. "Washington's Headquarters Valley Forge. Measured and Drawn." Valley Forge National Historical Park Archives, February, 1931.

2. Dodd, *Historic Structure Report*, p. 90.

CHAPTER FOUR: OWNERSHIP - FIRST 100 YEARS

1. Washington. *Writings.* ed. John CA Fitzpatrick, III. Boston and New York, 1925, p. 230.

2. Woodman. *Valley Forge.* p. 99.

3. James. M*emorial.* p. 221.

4. Woodman. *Valley Forge.* p. 99.

5. Dodd. *HSR. Bake House.* p. 2.

6. James. *Memorial.* p. 221.

7. Woodman, *Valley Forge.* p. 101.

8. Upper Merion "Window Pane Tax" Lists. Bulletin of the Historical Society of Montgomery County, Pennsylvania, XXIII (Norristown, PA., Fall, 1981) pp. 86-89.

9. James. *Memorial.* p. 224.

10. 1790 Census, Upper Merion Township. *Familysearch.org*.

11. James. *Memorial*. p. 225.

12. Woodman. *Valley Forge*. p. 103.

13. McDonald Powell, Barbara. "The Most Celebrated Encampment: Valley Forge in American Culture, 1777-1963." 1983. p. 61.

    _____. "Constitution of the Friendly Association for Mutual Interests, 1826." Historical Society of Pennsylvania. Ithaca, N.Y., University Microfilms International, 1983. p. 30.

14. Ibid., p. 29.

15. Woodman. *Valley Forge*. p. 100.

16. Dodd. *HSR*. p. 28.

17. Day. *Historical Collections of the State of Pennsylvania*. p. 496.

18. Lossing, *The Pictorial Field Book of the Revolution*. p. 332.

19. Ibid.

20. Day. *Historical Collections*. p. 496.

21. Woodman. *History of Valley Forge*. p. 100. James. p. 219.

22. Lossing, *Pictorial Field Book*. p. 332.

23. Ibid.

24. Dodd. *HSR. Washington's Headquarters.* Appendix A p.5; Montco Will 3209, Orphan's Court 9388.

25. Ibid., Montco Deed 77:632.

26. 1850 Census of Free Inhabitants, Upper Merion Township. *Familysearch.org.*

27. Statement made by Rev. Dr. William Powick at Valley Forge, July 19, 1929. Valley Forge National Historical Park Archives.

28. James. *Memorial.* p. 219.

CHAPTER FIVE: PUBLIC OWNERSHIP & RESTORATION ACTIVITY

1. Stager. *History of the Centennial and Memorial Association of Valley Forge, 1878-1910.* pp. 81-86.

2. Newspaper item, June 19, 1878.

3. *Proceedings on the Occasion of the Centennial Celebration of the Occupation of Valley Forge by the Continental Army Under George Washington, June 19, 1878. Also, Dedication of Headquarters, June 19, 1879.* J. B. Lippincott & Co., Philadelphia, 1879.

4. Dodd. *HSR. Washington's Headquarters.* Appendix A, p.6.

5. Montco Deed 252:83, 252:88, 306:67.

6. Stager. *Centennial and Memorial Association,* p. 114.

7. National Heritage Corporation. *Historical Research Report, Valley Forge State Park.* 1974. p. 51. Valley Forge National Historical Park Library. p. 56.

8. Jones, A. Conrad, Mrs., Letter to Horace Wells Sellers, Sellers Papers, Valley Forge National Historical Park Archives.

9. G. Edwin Brumbaugh, "Washington's Headquarters, Valley Forge, Pa." in Brumbaugh and G. Edwin Ruthrauff, "Report Regarding Architectural Services at Valley Forge Historical Park Prior to Administration by United States Department of Interior National Park Service." Valley Forge National Historical Park Library, May 31, 1980.

10. Stager. *Centennial and Memorial Association,* p. 184.

11. Reports of the Valley Forge Park Commission, 1912, Valley Forge National Historical Park Archives, p.19.

12. Ibid., 1910, p. 6.

13. Ibid., 1919, p. 5.

14. "House Beautiful," v1. 1xiii January, 1928, p. 98.

15. Horace Wells Sellers. "Memorandum of inspection of cuts in plaster in front room and hallway." Sellers Papers, Valley Forge National Historical Park Archives, February 14, 1931.

16. ____ "Supplementary Report on Headquarters House, Valley Forge." Sellers Papers, April 9, 1931, p. 3.

17. Ibid.

18. Dodd. *HSR. Washington's Headquarters.* Appendix K-1 to K-2. Brumbaugh to H. B. Wright, March 22, 1949.

19. Vance Packard. *Washington's Headquarters, Valley Forge.* Data from field notes on archaeological exploration, 1973.

20. Ibid.

21. "Picket Post." Valley Forge Historical Society, Winter, 1976. pp. 30-32.

22. Fish, Richard. "Master Report of Washington's Headquarters." February 9, 1976. Valley Forge National Historical Park Library, p. 10.

23. Ibid., p. 11.

24. Dodd. *HSR. Appendix M 1-6; N 1-4.*

25. _____. *Washington's Headquarters.* p. 61.

26. Ibid.

27. Treese. "Things That Tell the Story," Early American Life, June 1993. pp. 55-66.

SELECTED BIBLIOGRAPHY

Bining, Arthur Cecil. *Pennsylvania Iron Manufacture in the 18th Century*. 2nd ed. Pennsylvania Historic and Museum Commission, 1973.

Boudinot, Elias. *Journal or Historical Recollections of American Events During the Revolutionary War*. Philadelphia, PA., 1794.

Brumbaugh, G. Edwin. *Report Regarding Architectural Services at Valley Forge Historical Park prior to Administration by United States Department of Interior National Park Service.* Brumbaugh and Ruthrauff. Valley Forge National Historical Park Library, 1980.

Chastellux, François Jean (Marquis de). *Travels in North America in the Years 1780, 1781 and 1782*. Howard C. Rice, Jr., editor. University of North Carolina, 1963.

Day, Sherman. *Historical Collections of the State of Pennsylvania.* George W. Gorton, Philadelphia, 1843.

Dodd, John Bruce and Cherry. *Historic Structure Report: Part 4, Architectural Data, David Potts House, The Bake House.* Valley Forge National Historical Park. For the United States Department of the Interior, National Park Service, Mid Atlantic Region, 1981.

Dodd, John Bruce and Cherry. *Historic Structure Report: part 4, Architectural Data: Washington's Headquarters.* Valley Forge National Historical Park. For the United

States Department of the Interior, National Park Service, Mid Atlantic Region, 1981.

Fletcher, Stevenson Whitcomb. *Pennsylvania Agriculture and Country Life, 1640-1840.* Pennsylvania Historical and Museum Commission, Harrisburg, PA., 1950.

"Historical Research Valley Forge State Park." Prepared for the Pennsylvania Historical and Museum Commission. National Heritage Corporation, West Chester, PA., February 20, 1974.

James, Mrs. Thomas Potts. *Memorial of Thomas Potts, Junior, who Settled in Pennsylvania: with an Historic-genealogical Account of his Descendants to the Eighth Generation.* Privately printed, Cambridge, 1874.

Leckie, Robert. *George Washington's War, the Saga of the American Revolution.* Harper Perennial, 1993.

Lemon, James T. *The Best Poor Man's Country: A Geographical Study of Early Southeastern Pennsylvania.* W.W. Norton, 1972.

Lossing, Benson J. *The Pictorial Field-Book of the Revolution*, vol. II. Harper & Brothers, 1885. Reprint. Rutland, Vermont: C.E. Tuttle, 1972.

McDonald Powell, Barbara. "The Most Celebrated Encampment: Valley Forge in American Culture, 1777-1963." Ph.D. Dissertation, Cornell University, 1983.

_____. "Constitution of the Friendly Association for Mutual Interests, 1826." Historical Society of

Pennsylvania. Ithaca, N.Y., University Microfilms International, 1983.

Menz, Katherine B. *Historic Furnishings Report: Washington's Headquarters, Valley Forge National Historical Park.* National Park Service, 1989.

Millar, Donald. *Measured Drawings of some Colonial and Georgian Houses.* New York, 1916.

Proceedings on the Occasion of the Centennial Celebration of the Occupation of Valley Forge by the Continental Army Under George Washington, June 19, 1878. Also, Dedication of Headquarters, June 19, 1879. With an appendix. J. B. Lippincott & Co., Philadelphia, 1879.

Stager, H.J. *History of the Centennial and Memorial Association of Valley Forge, 1878-1910.* National Park Service, 1911.

Stone, Garry Wheeler. "The Mount Joy Forge on Valley Creek." *The Scope of Historical Archaeology, essays in honor of John L. Cotter.* Edited by David G. Orr and Daniel G. Crozier. Temple University, 1984.

Treese, Lorett. *Valley Forge Making and Remaking a National Symbol.* Pennsylvania State University Press, 1995.

_____ "Things That Tell the Story," Early American Life, June 1993. pp. 55-66.

Washington, George. *The Writings of George Washington from the Original Manuscript Sources, 1745-1799, Volume 27.* John Clement Fitzpatrick, ed. U. S. Government Printing Office, 1931.

Woodman, Henry. *The History of the Valley Forge.* Privately published. John Francis, Sr. Oaks, PA., 1922.

ILLUSTRATIONS

Abbreviations:
HQ   Washington's Headquarters
VFNHP   Valley Forge National Historical Park

Page *Description*
    Cover photograph of HQ
      Jeffrey Buehner
    Photograph of HQ
      Jeffrey Buehner

PREFACE

 2 Washington's Headquarters in VFNHP
      Jeffrey Buehner

CHAPTER ONE

 6 Aerial view of Valley Forge – 2018
      Google Maps
11 Chart of Potts family, part I
      Ancestry.com and
      James, Memorial of Thomas Potts, Junior
13 Chart of Potts family, part II
16 Map of John Potts' Mill Tract property north of Gulph Road
      Dodd. Historic Structure Report. 1981, p. 52
17 Map of Valley Forge prior to the Revolution
      Stone. The Mount Joy Forge on Valley Creek. p.111,
      labels added by James R. Bachman
22 Southeast view showing chimney caps
      Jeffrey Buehner

CHAPTER TWO

31	Map of location of Military Operations, fall 1777	
	Stone. The Mount Joy Forge on Valley Creek. p. 86, labels added by James R. Bachman	
43	Baron Friedrich Wilhelm von Steuben, 1730-1794	
	Google Images	
46	General George Washington and Marquis de Lafayette at Valley Forge	
	Google images – Library of Congress	
48	Huts at Valley Forge	
	Google Images	
52	Map of Encampment at Valley Forge by Louis Duportail	
	Google Images	
58	Washington's HQ, second floor plan	
	Menz. *Historic Furnishings Report, p. 4*	
59	Washington's HQ, first floor plan	
	Menz. *Historic Furnishings Report, p. 3*	

CHAPTER THREE

62	Drawing of Potts house – first floor plan	
	by James R. Bachman based on L.H. Sellers' drawings	
63	Drawing of Potts house – second floor plan	
	Ibid.	
64	Drawing of west elevation (façade)	
	James R. Bachman, copy from drawing in Millar, Donald. Measured drawings of some Colonial and Georgian Houses. New York, 1916.	
64	Drawing of east elevation (rear)	
	James R. Bachman, copy from drawing in Millar, Measured drawings	
65	Drawing of north elevation	
	James R. Bachman, copy from drawing in Millar, Measured drawings	

66	Dogtrot looking west
	Jeffrey Buehner
67	Dogtrot at Wentz House
	James R. Bachman
68	Drawing of Palladian pediment
	James R. Bachman
68	Drawing of south elevation
	James R. Bachman, copy from drawing in Millar, Measured drawings
70	Drawing of stonework patterns
	James R. Bachman
72	Parlor showing door to vestibule
	Michael Cerwinka
73	Dining room showing door to vestibule
	Michael Cerwinka
75	Second floor plan, front bedroom, Martha's sitting room?
	Michael Cerwinka
75	Another view of second floor, front bedroom
	Michael Cerwinka
76	Second floor, back bedroom
	Michael Cerwinka
80	Photograph of cornice
	Jeffrey Buehner
80	Drawing of cornice
	James R. Bachman
81	Double quirked bead
	Google images
83	Drawing of window sash
	James R. Bachman, copy from drawing in Millar, Measured drawings
84	Drawing of mortise and tenon joint
	James R. Bachman
85	Exterior view of window and shutters
	Jeffrey Buehner
87	Dining room paneling with windows and open cabinet
	Michael Cerwinka
88	Second floor back bedroom – detail paneling
	Michael Cerwinka
89	Parlor paneling, detail of doorway to vestibule moldings
	Michael Cerwinka

89	China cabinet (in red) in the parlor
	Michael Cerwinka
90	Close up of imbalance in paneling
	Phillip Wallace. Colonial Houses,
	Pre-Revolutionary Period.
	Philadelphia, 1931
91	Parlor paneling showing imbalance above china cabinet
	James R. Bachman
92	Parlor paneling imbalance above china cabinet
	Phillip Wallace. Colonial Houses,
	Pre-Revolutionary Period.
	Philadelphia, 1931
95	Drawing of detail of floor structure
	James R. Bachman
96	Drawing of detail of plasterwork (cutaway view)
	James R. Bachman

CHAPTER FOUR

106	Table -Federal Direct Tax, 1798 – Upper Merion "Window Pane Tax"
	"Bulletin of the Historical Society,"
	Pennsylvania, XXIII,
	Norristown, PA., Fall 1981, pp. 86-89
108	Chart of children of Isaac Potts & Martha Bolton
	Ancestry.com
115	Engraving of 1840, showing one-story log cabin wing
	VFNHP archives
116	Engraving of 1843, showing full two-story wing by Sherman Day
	Day. Historical Collections of the
	State of Pennsylvania
116	Sketch of HQ by Benson Lossing, 1852
	Lossing, The Pictorial Field-Book of the
	Revolution. 1851, Chapter XIII, p. 332
119	Print of stereopticon with HQ in background, 1859
	VFNHP archives
119	First known photograph taken in 1861 by Lewis Horning
	Courtesy VFNHP

120	Sketch of residence of Isaac Potts at Valley Forge
	(Washington HQ) – pre 1874
		James. Memorial of Thomas Potts, Junior, p. 217

CHAPTER FIVE

125	Picture of Anna Morris Holstein
		FindaGrave.com. Photo added by John Hennigar
127	Cornerstone
		Jeffrey Buehner
131	Drawing of 1888 wing revision
		James R. Bachman,
		copy from drawing by L.H. Sellers, 1931
131	Drawing of wing floor plan 1888 until 1934
		James R. Bachman. Ibid.
132	Log cabin addition from southeast after 1888 restoration
		VFNHP archives
132	Log cabin addition from northwest after 1888 restoration
		VFNHP archives
134	Drawing of brick arch, *ca.* 1888
		James R. Bachman
139	Warden standing by HQ, *ca.* 1900
		VFNHP archives
149	View showing wing with dogtrot eliminated and
	full two stories, 1952
		James R. Bachman
151	Dining room picture from postcard, *ca.* 1950, showing
	Brumbaugh colors
		VFNHP archives
151	Approximate color swatches selected by Brumbaughs
		Dodd. HSR. Paint research by E.G. Brumbaugh
		James R. Bachman, Benjamin Moore's historical
		paint
152	HQ with cannon as of 1954
		VFNHP archives
156	Drawing of original floor level of kitchen wing –
	1976 restoration
		James R. Bachman, as described in Dodd, HSR
159	Kitchen wing from north with beehive oven
		Jeffrey Buehner

159	View from northwest of 1976 restoration
	James R. Bachman
160	Headquarters' stable showing arched opening
	James R. Bachman
161	Drawing of elevation of 1976 restored wing
	James R. Bachman, copy from drawing by
	L.H. Sellers
162	Kitchen as it is today
	Michael Cerwinka
163	Drawing of details of rake boards of north and south gable before 1976
	James R. Bachman
163	Drawing of pointing of mortar joints in 1976
	James R. Bachman
164	Rear view of house showing trap door
	James R. Bachman
165	Drawing of basement plan
	James R. Bachman, copy from drawing by
	L.H. Sellers
167	South end showing foundation stones exposed in re-grading in 1976
	Jeffrey Buehner
169	Northwest corner of main house showing foundation stones exposed in 1976
	James R. Bachman

EPILOGUE

173	Southwest view of HQ
	Jeffrey Buehner

INDEX

American Military
- Lee, General Charles, *44, 55, 57*
- Lee, Colonel Henry ("light-horse Harry"), *35*
- Gates, Horatio, *40*
- Gibbs, Caleb, special aide to General Washington, *44, 50*
- Greene, Nathanael, Quartermaster General, *43*
- Hamilton. Colonel Alexander, *35, 50*
- Knox, General Henry, battle of Germantown, *39*
- Lewis, George, aide and nephew of General Washington, *50*
- Mifflin, Thomas, Quartermaster General, *26*
- Potter, General in Washington's army, *34*
- Tilghman, Tench, aide to General Washington, *50, 54*
- Washington, George, Commander in Chief,
    - appropriates Potts house, *23*
    - Christmas Day in headquarters, *48*
    - personal criticism, *41*
    - rooms in headquarters, *58,*59
    - touring old grounds, *97*

Bean, Theodore, restoration committee, *134, 138,, 145*
Biddle, Clement, chief of baggage, *32;*
    letter to General Washington regarding supplies, *32, 34*
Boudinot, Elias, *55, 57*
Brandywine Creek, *30, 38*
British Military
- Burgoyne, General, *28, 29*
- Clinton, Sir Henry, General, *43, 44*
- Cornwallis, General Charles, *30, 34, 36*
- Howe, General William, *8, 25, 27, 30,37-38,41, 46, 47*
    - seaborne expedition, *29;*
    - relieved of command, *43*
- Knyphausen, Wilhem von, commanding British forces, *34*

Brumbaugh, G. Edwin, architect, *135, 138, 150-153, 166*
Brumbaugh, Frances, interior decorator, *150-152*

census 1790, *108, 110;* 1850, *121*
Chastellux, Marquis de, *57*
Centennial and Memorial Association of Valley Forge, *129*
Chew, Justice Benjamin, Chew house, capture of, *39*
Colebrookdale Furnace, *10*
Continental Congress, *25, 35, 37, 50*
cornerstone, *126-127*

Daughters of the American Revolution, D.A.R., *137*
Day, Sherman, 1843 engraving, *116-120, 133, 144, 149*
Dewees, William, *19- 20, 26-27, 32, 34-35, 37, 104, 112*
    letter from Biddle, *32*
    bankruptcy, *99*
Dodd, John Bruce and Cherry, *see* Historic Structure Report
Drinker, Elizabeth, *54, 55*
Duportail, Louis, French engineer, *see* maps

Free and Accepted Masons, *127*
Friendly Association for Mutual Interests, *113*

Germantown, *30, 38 ,40, 103*
Gulph Mills, *47*

Hallowell, R.T.S., architect, *130*
Hewes, Caleb, second husband of Deborah, *24*
Hewes, Deborah, rents Potts house, *23, 44, 49*
Historic structure report, *146, 167*
Holstein, Anna Morris, *125- 126*
Holstein, William, husband of Anna, *127, 128*
huts, size and number of, *48*

Isaac, son of John Potts Sr., *see* Potts, Isaac
Isabella, Mrs. Thomas Potts James,
    see James, Mrs. Thomas Potts

James, Jonathan, *53*
James, Mrs. Thomas Potts, Isabella, historian of Potts
    family, *10, 21,53, 107, 110, 119, 124*
Jones, Mrs. A. Conrad, daughter of Bean, Theodore, *134*

Jones, James, member of the Harmonist experiment, *113, 114, 134, 164;*
 will, *121*

Kitchen wing, *113-124, 130-137, 154-162*

Laurens, John, volunteer aide, *50*
Lee, William "Billy", body servant to General Washington, *51*
Lossing, Benson, *116-122, 133, 144, 149;*
 visit to Potts house, *121*
Louis XVI, King (of France), *40*

Maps
 Encampment at Valley Forge, Louis Duportail, *52*
 Location of Military Operations, fall 1777, *31*
 Mill tract, location of headquarters and barnyard, *16*
 Forges of Potts and Dewees at Valley Forge, *17*
McGuire, Patrick, dismissal as steward, *51*
Monmouth, battle of Germantown, *44*
Montresor, Captain John, notebook, *35*
Mount Joy, *6, 35*
 Mount Joy Forge, *9, 12-14, 19, 26*
Mount Misery, *47*
Mount Vernon Ladies Association, *125*

National Heritage Corporation of West Chester,
 Pennsylvania, *153, 166*
National Park Service, *56, 157*
New Harmony, alternative life style, *see* Owen, Robert

Owen, Robert, alternative life style, Harmonist experiment, *112-113*

Packard, Vance, archeologist, *156-157*
Palladian pediment, *see* structural details
Palladio, Andrea, *68, 79*
Paneling, *see* structural details
Paoli, *36*
Paul, Jacob, acquiring estate, *103, 105*
Paul, Joseph, son of Jacob, *104, 113*
Patriotic Order Sons of America, *128, 138*

Penn, family tract, *9*
Pennsylvania Historical and Museum Commission, *153*
Pennypacker's Mill, *see* Schwenksville
Perkiomen Valley Creek, *34*
Pickering Creek, *36*
Potts, Isaac, *12, 17-23, 49, 53, 71, 99- 101, 103,107, 109-110, 112-113, 118, 120, 150, 174*
Pottsgrove, *10, 18, 20, 21, 24, 34, 49, 100*

race, *12, 19, 99*
Reading Furnace, *32*
Religious groups
    Anglicans, *7*
    Baptists, *7*
    German Lutherans, *7*
    Presbyterians, *7*
    Quakers, *7*
        Benezet, Anthony, *109*
        Drinker, Elizabeth, *54, 56*
        Exeter Meeting, *20, 100*
        Isaac and Martha, *20*
        Radnor meeting, *20*
Roads
    Baptist Road, *35*
    Great Road or Gulph Road, *15*
    Gulph Road, Highway 23, *6, 12, 15, 32, 35, 100, 104, 112, 118*
    Lancaster Road, Highway 30, *30*
    North Gulph Road, *6*
    Nutt Road, *35*
Rutter family, *9*

Saratoga, *40*
Savage family, *9*
Schwenksville, formerly Pennypacker, *37*
Sellers, Horace Wells, architect, *134, 143- 147, 154, 161, 168, 172*
Sheas, Jerome, Park superintendent, *147*
stereopticon, *118*
Steuben, Friedrich Wilhelm, Baron von, *43*

structural details, *94*
  cornice, *78-81, 87, 162*
  cyma, recta, reversa, *79*
  garret, low ceilinged attic, *50, 76, 111, 161*
  joinery, joiner, *78-87*
  micaceous sandstone, *69*
  mortise and tenon, *84, 94*
  muntin, divider, *82, 136*
  oculus, *23, 68, 71, 76, 119, 130, 136*
  ogee, *79, 80, 162*
  ovolo, *80-83, 86*
  Palladian pediment, *68*
  paneling, *73. 74, 77-83, 84-88. 90, 92-93, 96, 130, 151*
  pent eave, *68-70, 119, 130, 133, 146, 148, 158*
  plastering, plasterwork, *76, 93-94, 96, 146, 152*
  rabbet, *83*
  rubble, stone, *69-70*
  sash, window, *82-83, 119, 130, 136, 171*
  summer beam, *94-95*

Tax, Federal Direct, Glass, *105, 106, 118, 157*
Thomas Potts James, Mrs., *see* James
Ticonderoga, Fort, *28*

Upper Merion Township, *23*

Valley Forge Park Commission, established, *138*
Vergennes, Count de, French foreign minister, *40*

Warren, Mercy, *see* Washington, Martha
Warton, Thomas, Washington's letter regarding his steward, *51-52*
Warwick, *32, 34*
Washington, Martha, arrives at Valley Forge, *51*
      letter to Mercy Warren, *53-54*
     bedroom, *56-57*
     sitting room, *56-57*

water for mills, usage agreement, *19*

Wentz, Peter, house, *67, 146*
Whitemarsh, *39, 47*

Will, John Potts, Sr., *15*
      Isaac Potts, *109*
Woodman, Henry, historian, *99*

Yellow Springs, *32, 34*

Made in the
USA
Monee, IL